CONTEXTS

THE WORK OF HODDER AND PARTNERS

Published by RIBA Publishing, part of
RIBA Enterprises Ltd, The Old Post Office,
St Nicholas Street, Newcastle upon Tyne,
NE1 1RH

ISBN 978-1-85946-826-5

British Library
Cataloguing-in-Publication Data
A catalogue record for this book
is available from the British Library.

Editor: Professor Peter Walker
Commissioning Editor: Elizabeth Webster
Production: Philip Handley
Designed and typeset by
Thomas Manss & Company
Printed and bound by
Pureprint Group, Uckfield, UK

www.ribaenterprises.com

RIBA Publishing

CONTEXTS

THE WORK OF HODDER AND PARTNERS

IMAGE CREDITS

Bernard Cox / RIBA Collections 59
Dennis Gilbert 24–5, 56, 57, 91, 92, 94, 117, 118, 142, 143, 145, 146, 147
Daniel Hopkinson 30–1, 33, 60–1, 62–3, 70, 71, 72, 75, 82–3, 125, 156, 157
Greater Manchester Police 120
Hodder and Partners 27, 36, 40–1, 96–7, 110–11, 128–29, 130, 131
Infinite 3D 13, 32, 124
John Donat / RIBA Collections 51
Jonathan Moore 20–1, 52, 100–01, 135, 136, 137
L.S. Lowry A View from the Window of Royal Technical College, Salford, Looking Towards Manchester 1924 © The Lowry Collection, Salford 93
Martine Hamilton Knight 22, 26–7, 64, 65, 84, 103, 104, 106–7, 112–13, 140, 152, 153, 154–55
Peter Cook 9, 23, 26, 28, 29, 34, 35, 38, 39, 54, 55, 66–7, 67, 68–9, 70, 74, 76–7, 79, 81, 86, 87, 88, 90, 99, 123, 126–27, 138, 139, 141, 148, 149, 150, 151, 158–9, 159, 160–61, 162, 162–63
RIBA Publishing 42
Richard Davies 43
Richard Langendorf 48–9
Stephen Hodder 14, 16–7, 18
Tom Burnham 98
Tom Stoddart 116
Tom Stuart-Smith 109
Tony Chapman 108

CONTENTS

STEPHEN
HODDER

PREFACE

'...no man can build on the void, and a civilization that breaks with the style at its disposal soon finds itself empty-handed.'
André Malraux, *The Voices of Silence*, 1953

As I was venturing into practice in 1983, September's issue of *The Architectural Review* proclaimed an architecture of 'Romantic Pragmatism': an architecture that responds to the exigencies of brief and site, and that is informed by tradition but is not eclectic, responsive but not kitsch, gentle but not weak, systematic but not severe. It resonated with me, and ignited a restless process of inquiry and a personal search for a language of authenticity.

As with the work of the architects in that issue, my search has been concerned with the need to generate a humane architecture while drawing on the rational disciplines of modernism. It is a search that is concerned with enhancing the lives of people and attaining a sense of place.

More than 30 years later that restlessness remains, and I constantly challenge the influences on and question the relevance of our work in the canon of British architecture.

What follows is a critical examination of the work of the practice and its influences, and the contexts that have shaped this. Five writers on architecture – two of whom combine writing with practice – have written essays for this book, each of which looks at Hodder and Partners through a particular lens.

In Chapter 1, *Locating Hodder and Partners: The Business of Architecture*, Professor Peter Walker – also the Editor of this book – contextualises the practice's work against the seismic changes that have been experienced by the profession and the wider industry over the last 25 years.

In Chapter 2, *The Jacobsen Influence: Form, Texture, Detail and Landscape*, Hugh Pearman, Editor of the *RIBA Journal*, reflects on our 1992 extension to St Catherine's College, Oxford – Arne Jacobsen's masterpiece. The college has remained a client of the practice for many years, and the work has formed the backbone of our studio's output ever since. Jacobsen's buildings have had a constant presence and acted as a reference point in the development of our architectural approach and language.

In Chapter 3, *Spirit of Place: Latent Qualities in Architecture*, Tony Chapman examines physical context as a strong generator in the work of Hodder and Partners. A number of buildings are discussed in which the genesis of each building's design is seemingly a search for the essential qualities of a place.

In Chapter 4, *Hodder and Partners: A Manchester Practice*, Laura Mark parallels key moments in Manchester's remarkable renaissance in recent times with those of the practice. Were they fortuitous or planned?

Finally in Chapter 5, *Articulating Legibility, Craft, People and Places*, Rob Gregory interrogates the notion that the making of buildings underpins the work, and that this is not only a consideration of performance but one of construction legibility. The meticulous consideration of detail was perhaps ingrained in my early education, but does it represent continuity of the British Arts and Crafts tradition?

There are so many people to thank in the realisation of this book: the five authors, who each rose to the challenge of offering a different perspective on the same body of work, in particular Peter Walker who flattered me in agreeing to be Editor; Liz Webster, RIBA Publishing's Senior Commissioning Editor, who had the unenviable challenge of managing the whole process; the designer Thomas Manss, who was challenged to capture the spirit of our work in this object and exceeded this challenge; and of course to my marital and business partner, Claire, and everyone, architects, consultants, contractors and clients alike, who have enabled the work of Hodder and Partners.

Staircase detail, South residential pavilion, St Clare's, Oxford

PETER WALKER

LOCATING HODDER AND PARTNERS: THE BUSINESS OF ARCHITECTURE

"“You know, father, what I should really like to be –
I should like to be an architect.”
“Should ye?” said his father, who attached no importance of any kind to this avowal of a preference. “Well, what you want is a bit o' business training for a start, I'm thinking.”'
Arnold Bennett, *Clayhanger*, 1910

In 1953 the then President of the RIBA, Howard Robertson, wrote the short pamphlet *The Architect and his Work*, which he described as a guide for clients to the services to expect from an architect. Sixty years later, in 2013, Stephen Hodder became President of the RIBA, and on the conclusion of his presidency published *Client & Architect: Developing the Essential Relationship*.

In these 60 years much has changed in the practice of architecture. The 1953 pamphlet was an inward-looking analysis of the architect's role, confidently describing a fixed process from brief to building handover, carried out in a well-understood sequence within an established client–architect relationship. The roles were clear – architects designed, builders built and clients paid, and the hierarchy was also clear – the architect was top of the pile.

The 2013 publication was by contrast an outward-looking and inclusive discussion of a less certain relationship between architect and client, and between architect and builder.

And in essence this is the story of architectural practice – of the business of architecture – in the second half of the 20th century and at the start of the 21st century: the gradual but steady shift from the omnipotent, all-controlling architect designing every detail, specifying every component and closely over-seeing the building contract, to a more complicated client–architect relationship. Changes in forms of building procurement have forced a rethinking of the architect's way of working, and have also changed the relationship to the client and the builder – who is often now, at least for part of the commission, also the client. This creates a contractual context for making buildings in which the control of the design is more slippery. The architect is required to find ways to maintain the quality of the architecture as it passes through many hands and crosses many contractual barriers on the journey from idea to building.

Stephen Hodder first set up in practice in 1983, exactly at the mid-point of this cycle. Up until then much was as it had always been; what began around this time was a period of significant, rapid and far-reaching change in the role and status of the architect. All the early Hodder buildings were carried out on traditional contracts; by contrast almost all the recent work is built using some form of design and build or construction management contract.

Maintaining critical practice in the context of these changing relationships has been the challenge for architects in these times. And what of the place?

Manchester is very much the place of Hodder and Partners. The office occupies a site between the Bridgewater Canal – a tributary of the Manchester Ship Canal – and a railway viaduct enduring artefacts of the Industrial Revolution that give Manchester its built exoskeleton. The office occupies the ground floor of a fashionable block of apartments in a once industrial, then derelict, but now revived area of Manchester: an example of the Manchester of now, where living in the city has returned as a way of life.

Inside the office everything is black and white: the furniture white (Italian, of course) and the clothes black. For these are architects – and more precisely, modern architects. A linear entrance hall is lined with building models and framed awards – evidence of architecture laboured over successfully.

There is something entirely appropriate about the place – for Hodder and Partners is categorically a Manchester practice, and Stephen Hodder is both a product and significant producer of Manchester.

Hodder and Partners office, Kelso Place, Manchester, from the Bridgewater Canal

hodder+partners

One way of telling the story of Hodder and Partners is by reference to the built output; another way is by reference to the practice and the way of working. One story is concerned with product, the other with process. So what might an examination of the process – the practice and the people – illuminate?

The architect and his office

Stephen Hodder was born in Stockport in what is now Greater Manchester. After a childhood in Nottinghamshire he moved back to Manchester to take up a place at the School of Architecture, University of Manchester, from where he graduated in 1981 with a Distinction in the Bachelor of Architecture degree. After graduation he joined Building Design Partnership (BDP), at that time probably the leading – certainly by size – architectural practice in the north of England. BDP was (and is) a well-respected firm, and in many ways typical of the large architectural practices of the time, although set up as a multidisciplinary organisation, which was unusual then, and is still unusual today. As a newly qualified architect Hodder could have settled down and put his energy into climbing the corporate ladder, but in his own words he was 'ambitious and impatient'. What BDP could offer him was an established, structured, traditional architectural practice turning out some fine work. Although this was for many young architects exactly the supportive environment they would have wanted in their early career, it would not allow Hodder the kind of control – both architectural and commercial – he impatiently sought.

Architectural practice in the 1980s was different from architectural practice now – not just in detail, but fundamentally. Almost all architectural practices traded either as sole practitioners or as a partnership. Those working at the practice who were not partners were referred to as assistants – a language that firmly established the partners both as owners of the business and as authors of the work of the practice, whether that was true or not. The physical landscape of the office was typically an open-plan space filled with drawing boards, with the partners' cellular office(s) either to one side or, in bigger organisations such as BDP, in spacious offices on the top floor. The partner – having taken the room at the top – became less architect and more manager, with the adjustable drawing board permanently on the horizontal plane to provide a convenient surface for piles of architects' instructions, building contracts, letters awaiting signature and, most importantly, fee invoices.

It was also a time when architects drew every plan, every section and every detail by hand. Hodder recalls with affection honing his drafting and lettering skills, and daily battles to stop the Rotring pen from clogging up – in the pursuit of drawings that could be more than just a means of explaining a design to the builder, but rather works of art in themselves. This was also the time when buildings were procured by 'the traditional method' – a process in which architects administered the terms of the construction contract from the start on site to handover to client, with complete control over the realisation of the design.

The act of producing architecture and being an architect was demanding of both time and knowledge. Expectations of complete technical drawings and specifications before the start of construction placed unrealistic demands on inexperienced architects who, in the absence of any early input from the builder, relied on the building suppliers' reps to guide them. At the same time, architects

Staircase 17,
St Catherine's College, Oxford,
Phase II, pencil on detail paper

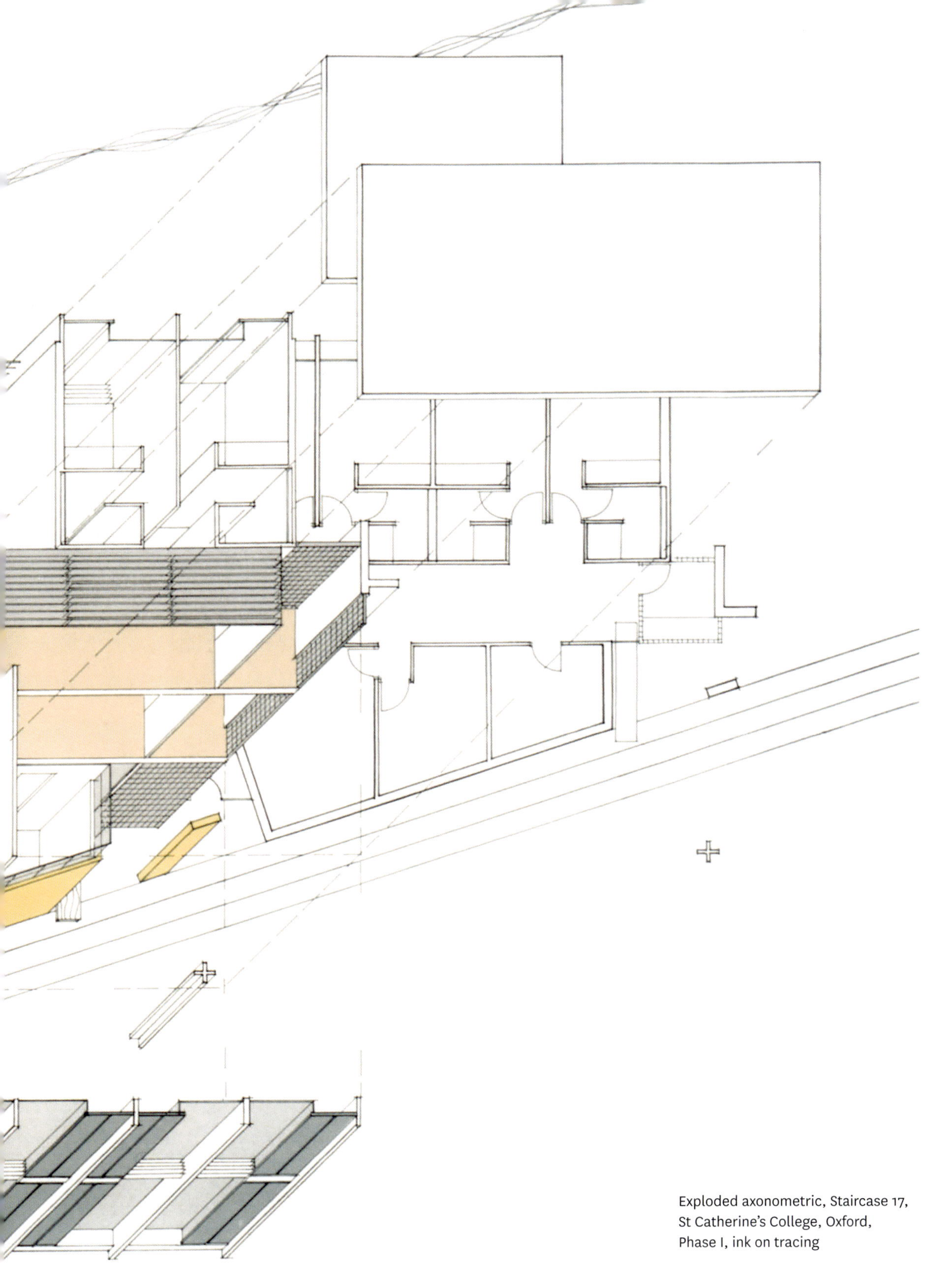

Exploded axonometric, Staircase 17, St Catherine's College, Oxford, Phase I, ink on tracing

required a firm grasp of construction contract law, and the ability to clear the regulatory hurdles of planning and building regulations approval. The post-university apprenticeship that architects went through to develop these skills was an important part of professional development, and a rite of passage usually carried out in an established practice. But the young Hodder was in too much of a hurry to hang around for this.

In 1983 he set up, with Michael Lees, the Hodder Lees Partnership – the two had been together in the final year at university just two years earlier. The practice initially worked from Hodder's house in Goosnargh near Preston for 15 months, during which time it won the competition to repurpose Lytham Station. Coincidentally, the competition panel was chaired by a former boss, Sir George Grenfell-Baines, the founding Chairman of BDP.

The young practice picked up where Manchester University and BDP had left off, and the pair largely taught themselves the architect's trade, although Hodder acknowledges the avuncular support of the engineers, quantity surveyors and contractors they worked with.

This was certainly not the easiest way for a young architect to learn the ways of the business, but as Hodder notes, it meant that lessons were well learned. In the absence of any senior partner to consult, initiative, adaptability and a precocious confidence were key to their success. These characteristics, alongside a tenacious persistence, are qualities Hodder has been regularly required to draw on during his career as architect, as Chairman of Hodder and Partners, and as President of the RIBA from 2013 to 2015.

The practice eventually relocated to a converted former bank manager's house in Lytham, an upmarket seaside resort in Lancashire, and four years later moved to Manchester. Hodder points out that one reason for the move was the difficulty of luring talented young architects to a practice in sleepy, genteel Lytham.

The practice became Hodder Associates in 1992 and had immediate success – that year winning the Royal Fine Art Commission/Sunday Times Building of the Year award for Colne Swimming Pool in Lancashire. The building was on a site adjoining the work of Nicholas Grimshaw, who was at that time preoccupied with what came to be known as the hi-tech movement. Hodder's building was in a different tradition, however. It was less concerned with expressive tectonics, with a greater attention to the specifics of place – the Lancashire landscape familiar to Hodder.

St Catherine's College, Oxford, Phase I, from Napper's Bridge, ink on tracing

Overleaf:
Looking down Albert Road towards Colne Swimming Pool, Lancashire

Sports Centre

Oxford and Salford

A Fellow of St Catherine's College, Oxford spotted the press coverage of the Colne Swimming Pool award in a Sunday newspaper and invited Hodder to take part in a limited competition to extend Arne Jacobsen's Grade I-listed college building. Hodder Associates won the competition and so, from such a chance encounter, began a client relationship which continued for nearly 20 years.

In 1996 Hodder Associates was the first winner of the Stirling Prize, which has since become established as the most important award in British architecture. The award was for the Centenary Building at the University of Salford.

Oxford and Salford are two very different English cities – indeed Oxford University and Salford University are two very different English universities. Hodder demonstrated an ability to both read and respond to the place – one the formal, sylvan setting of an Oxford College as reinvented by Arne Jacobson; the other a run-down inner-city site tucked away among factories and local authority housing – and to respond to the very different clients. Salford University is a former Royal College of Technology given university status in 1967, and Oxford University is, well, Oxford: a world-renowned university made up of powerful independent colleges. Salford University was established during a period of expansion in UK universities in the 1960s. These new universities commissioned a roll-call of leading British architects of the time – Denys Lasdun at the University of East Anglia in Essex, Farmer and Dark at the University of Kent, Basil Spence at the

Staircase 17,
St Catherine's College, Oxford,
Phase I

Left:
Arumugam Building,
St Catherine's College, Oxford,
Phase II

Overleaf:
West elevation, Centenary Building,
University of Salford

University of Sussex, and RMJM at the University of Ulster – and came to be known collectively by their architecture as 'the plate glass universities' – younger siblings of the red-brick civic universities.

Salford was already an established campus but, as part of this expansion of higher education, needed new buildings and was imaginative enough to commission a young local practice. Although it is tempting to characterise Hodder Associates as a northern architectural practice, skilled in solving the wicked problems of messy post-industrial inner-city sites, this would be simplistic – or at least not the whole story. The ability to understand and negotiate the complex politics of an Oxford college and to respond intelligently to a unique established setting are also qualities that Hodder revealed, and which can be seen in later work including St Clare's, Oxford, the National Wildflower Centre at Knowsley, and the competition-winning RHS Garden Bridgewater at Worsley in Salford.

At both Oxford and Salford the relationship with the client was direct – Hodder was appointed by the university (or college) to prepare the design, produce the working drawings, and organise and oversee the building contract through to handover to the client. This relationship allowed for development of the brief in dialogue with the client, and close control of the realisation of the building on site; it also allowed for a response to changes introduced as the project developed – something that proved important on the Centenary Building, where the client's brief changed significantly during the design of the building. Although alternative 'design and build' ways of contracting for buildings were emerging at this time, these were not (yet) the way university buildings were procured.

St Clare's, Oxford, looking towards the 1903 Henry T. Hare Arts & Crafts house

National Wildflower Centre, Knowsley

Below:
The welcome building, RHS Garden Bridgewater

Manchester and beyond

At the end of the 1990s Hodder Associates was becoming well established as an award-winning practice, among the bright stars of English architecture.

An exciting new commission came up in 1996 for a new leisure centre and swimming pool in Stoke Newington in London – the Clissold Centre. This innovative and imaginative building was to be the key component in the regeneration of this run-down part of north London, and as a result, Hodder opened a London office, which operated until the completion of the project in 2002.

At the same time as Clissold was in design, back in Manchester two small but significant projects were completed.

The CUBE gallery, completed in 1998, was principally an Architecture Centre; part of a developing network of such centres throughout the UK, it was located in a Grade II-listed former cotton warehouse – a common Manchester building type. Building, place and function were all close to Hodder's heart and, in his words, the refurbishment and conversion of the two floors making up the gallery sought to 'add a further contemporary layer to the historic framework'. The space was owned and managed by the University of Salford, and in a large-scale reorganisation of the university driven by financial difficulties, CUBE was closed in October 2013.

Earlier, in June 1996, the IRA had detonated a massive bomb in Manchester city centre, which injured 220 people and destroyed a number of buildings. The shattered footbridge which had previously connected two shopping centres became one of the most vivid images of the bombing. As part of the rebuilding of the city centre, an architectural competition was held for a replacement bridge, which Hodder won, and

Entrance, CUBE gallery, Manchester

Corporation Street footbridge, Manchester

he was awarded the commission to design the new Corporation Street Footbridge. The striking form of the bridge – a glazed rotated hyperbolic paraboloid – is the result of a close collaboration between Hodder and the structural engineer Arup. The bridge is a small but beautifully realised piece that is both a sculptural symbol of the rebuilding of Manchester, and an important urban connection. Writing in *l'Arca* in 2000, Mario Arnaboldi noted: 'This project has turned into a sort of landmark for the city of Manchester, a sort of memorial to the bomb attack and a cutting-edge symbol of modernity and the city's culture.'

Changing times

At the start of the 21st century everything moved up the scale – in particular with regard to the height of the buildings Hodder was involved with – and everything changed in terms of procurement, the type of client and the relationship with the client, both contractual and organisational.

In the period following the Second World War, the British government embarked on a programme to create more homes to replace Victorian and Georgian inner-city slums, and to fill the vacant sites left after the Luftwaffe's bombing campaign. The story of what followed is well known: the downward spiral of technical failures and social problems found in the high-rise flats combined to give living in the city a bad name – something the British had always been a bit lukewarm about anyway. After a period of lost nerve, which saw the rise of something strangely described as 'vernacular architecture', in the 2000s British architects rediscovered building high, and British people rediscovered living in the city.

Manchester's skyline, showing the 37-storey Great Marlborough Street student accommodation

city tower
portland tower

However, this time it was not the local councils who were promoting and funding the building work, but private developers. Fuelled by low interest rates, the buy-to-let market sprang up. Developers, seeing an opportunity, particularly in cities with big student populations, began a programme of high-rise building that transformed the skyline of many British cities – and none more so than Manchester.

During this time Hodder and Partners designed a number of significant commercial and residential high-rise developments. In Manchester there was 4 Piccadilly Place (2009), Great Marlborough Street (2012), Motel One (2014) and Cambridge Street (2016). Across the Pennines in Sheffield there was St Paul's Place (2016), a large mixed-use development in the city centre. The residential towers ranged from 28 to 33 storeys, with the highest yet to be built in 2017 – the Ovatus project, which at 50 storeys will be the highest building in Liverpool. When reflecting on this collection, Hodder wryly points out that he suffers from vertigo.

All these developments were carried out using design and build contracts, in which Hodder and Partners was appointed by the client – a property developer – to prepare the initial design and obtain planning permission, and was then passed on by novation of the appointment contract to the building contractor to prepare the production information.

This has become the way things are done for large developments. It is a process that shifts commercial risk from developer to contractor, but it also creates a fracture in the client–architect relationship. Hodder notes that 'whether by the careful selection of contractor, or our "tenacious" approach, we have always retained a close, albeit non-contractual, relationship with the client post-novation. It can give

Great Marlborough Street
from the south

Left:
4 Piccadilly Place, Manchester

rise to tensions, but I believe we have a responsibility to express concern directly if the original design intent is in danger of being diluted. We are always keen not to completely fracture that essential relationship'. Hodder and Partners' considerable success in adapting to this form of working is centred on what Hodder describes as 'our inclusive collaborative approach, which recognises that whilst the relationship between architect and client is essential, so is that with the contractor'.

The landscape of the architect's office and the landscape in which the architect works – the wider project context – have changed. These changes have inevitably required architects to fundamentally rethink the business of being an architect; the way they work both to create a viable commercial operation, and to retain control of the design and realisation of their buildings. In the 25 years that Hodder and Partners has been around, it has had to navigate this changing landscape and continue to successfully reconcile commercial and critical practice.

For architects of Hodder's generation, CAD was something that came along once they had established careers (after a number of false dawns with clumsy software). And, like many of his contemporaries, Hodder freely admits to being CAD illiterate. This technology creates a new relationship between design idea and design drawing, but Hodder points out that 'I can still sketch every building in the office' – note the key words 'I' (personal control), 'still' (despite changing times) and 'sketch' (the tool of the trade).

It would not be possible for the practice to produce the vast numbers of production drawings and specifications for the complex large buildings Hodder is now designing without CAD and, more recently, without building information modelling (BIM).

No.1 Cambridge Street, Manchester, juxtaposed with Medlock Mill

Motel One, Manchester

St Paul's Place, Sheffield

The move from complete control of the design detail, together with the increasing use of off-site manufacture, requires a new way of working. Managing this scale of projects and the office required to produce them while maintaining critical practice creates new organisational challenges. This is a long way from three men in a terraced house in Lytham churning out hand-drawn details one step ahead of the contractor.

Hodder describes the design process in the office as 'inclusive' and 'based on the university crit system'. Design at Hodder and Partners takes place through frequent and constant reviews – formal and informal – and a constant conversation about architecture within the office. A medium-sized office with a small management team of Hodder as Chairman, Claire Hodder as Managing Director and two Associate Directors, Tom Goldthorpe and Matt Dawson, allows for a contained, light-on-the-feet design and management structure.

Claire Hodder joined Hodder Associates in 2004 and became Managing Director of the newly incorporated Hodder and Partners in 2008. Claire first worked at Michael Hyde and Associates, moving in 1997 to work with Austin-Smith:Lord. In 2000 she became an Associate with Aedas, focusing on transportation projects including Hyde Bus Station, Metrolink Phase 3 and a masterplan study for expansion of Manchester Airport.

Supply and demand in UK architecture is unbalanced – possibly a lasting effect of the 2008 recession, which has led to the fragmentation of larger practices into smaller ones. There is an oversupply of architectural firms, and this manifests itself in a constant downward pressure on fees, fierce competition for the best commissions and a challenging business environment. Claire's role as

Ovatus I and II residential towers in Liverpool, at a significant gateway to Liverpool Waterfront

Managing Director of Hodder and Partners has been to manage the business and to oversee large projects; a happy division of labour that has allowed Hodder to focus on design leadership and to pursue his interests outside the practice, in particular as President of the RIBA.

Although the type and scale of the projects has grown overall, there is still room for smaller, more delicate interventions, such as stitching together an existing context, as in the extension to St Clare's, Oxford, or redefining and reinventing a historic setting at RHS Garden Bridgewater in Worsley. Hodder finds himself back in familiar territory in Oxford and Salford.

Art studio, St Clare's, Oxford, from the Banbury Road

Right:
Warden's Lodge, and front of Henry T. Hare's Arts and Crafts house at St Clare's, Oxford

A public life beyond the office

Stephen Hodder – in appearance, in manner, in the way he speaks – is very much the architects' architect: a committed practitioner driven to build, immersed in his work and his office. But on the other hand there is the civic life of Stephen Hodder – the skilled and tenacious political operator.

In 2013 Hodder became President of the RIBA. For him this was not the result of a whimsical desire to trade on his reputation; neither was it a gratuitous desire for power or status. He had served his time in the Institute as a member of the Education Committee and Conservation Steering Group, and had served as Vice President for Membership, Nations and Regions. Beyond Portland Place he had been Chairman of the RIBA North West region and President of the Manchester Society of Architects.

So why would an award-winning architect, passionate about making buildings, with a full order book and more than enough to be getting on with, want to be President of the RIBA? When asked this,

19
03

Interior of the welcome building,
RHS Garden Bridgewater

Hodder referred to giving something back to the profession, to a desire to raise the public profile of architecture, and made the point that 'the profession, education and practice form a triangle, all three sides of which are important to me'.

In an interview at the time he became President, Hodder – ever the pragmatist, and ever impatient to get things done – said: 'I want to focus on a few small things and do them well.' In practice there were three things he chose to focus on – the evolving client–architect relationship, the creation of an Architecture Gallery at Portland Place, and the reform of architectural education – hardly small things.

Hodder took over the RIBA presidency at a difficult time both for architects and for the Institute – the economy was just coming out of recession and the profession was depressed. Hodder also had to deal with the fallout of 'Palestinegate' – an ill-judged excursion by the RIBA into global politics. Closer to home there was the need to resolve corporate governance and staff management issues at Portland Place. But he did get his three 'small things' done, or at least set them in motion – for these are things that are perhaps never truly 'done'.

The *Client & Architect* report has its roots in the *Strategic Study of the Profession* led by Frank Duffy in 1994, during his term as RIBA President. It can be seen as part of a continuum that goes back to the *Architect and His Work* of 1953, *The Architect and His Office* of 1958, the *Architect in the Construction Industry* of 1989 and *The Future for Architects?* of 2011, all part of a search by architects to redefine, influence and respond to changes in what Hodder's report refers to as 'the essential relationship'.

Front cover, *Client & Architect: developing the essential relationship*

The Architecture Gallery, RIBA,
by Carmody Groarke

The Architecture Gallery, designed by Carmody Groarke, is a place where drawings, photographs and models from the RIBA's permanent collection can be publicly displayed for the first time at Portland Place. Skilfully carved out of a service lightwell and disused offices, it creates visual links from the ground floor into spaces previously unseen by the public, and brings people into the building and into an engagement with architecture, exactly as Hodder hoped it would.

The reform of education that was embarked on during Hodder's presidency is undoubtedly the biggest rethink of architectural education since the Oxford Conference of 1958, and is by no measure a 'small thing'. Led by RIBA Director of Education David Gloster, the reforms involved extensive consultation with architects, students, academics and clients, described by Hodder as 'the most rigorous and collaborative review of architectural education in 50 years'. Although the practice of architecture has greatly changed in that time, the mix of practical and academic training that leads to qualification as an architect has changed little since Hodder was at Manchester University, and he makes the point that 'the current model of architectural education has been with us since the Oxford Conference'. The central proposal is a move to a seven-year course that integrates academic study and professional experience, with academic credits available for work-based learning.

Architecture in the UK has always been predominantly male, white and middle class – a situation perpetuated by an expensive and lengthy process of qualification. A desire to make education more practice-focused and to widen access to the profession were two concerns that drove these reforms. This is not the act of a practitioner President nostalgically recalling his university days, or misguidedly imagining – as many before have – that he has the panacea to architectural education (which would by extension solve all of the problems of British architecture).

When it comes to education, Hodder is no dilettante – he has combined teaching and practice throughout his working life, has written and lectured widely, has been an external examiner at a number of schools of architecture, and has been a Visiting Professor at the Birmingham School of Architecture, the Belfast School of Architecture and, since 2017, Visiting Professor in Architecture at the University of Salford. These were not empty honorary titles given by architecture departments to a Stirling Prize winner in an act of mutual vanity. Like many a young practitioner, Hodder had taught in studio for many years, in his case at the Manchester School of Architecture. When offered a Visiting Chair position at the Belfast School of Architecture he only accepted when the Head of School assured him that there was indeed a proper job for him to do. And over the four years of this appointment Hodder was a regular visiting critic and tutor in the design studio.

The architect and his work

Hodder and Partners is of a particular place – Manchester – and a particular time: 1992 to 2017. This 25-year period has been a time of huge change for architects, for the construction industry, and for post-industrial British cities. Much of the change has amounted to a steady reduction in the influence of the architect. Shifting professional boundaries have eroded the scope of the architect's work, and new forms of building procurement have moved the architect from the demand side to the supply side and, as a result, made the client–architect relationship more remote.

The use of CAD and BIM in design has enabled greater efficiency – bigger buildings can be designed in a smaller office – but this has also reduced the immediacy of the brain–hand–sketchpad nexus.

The relationship of society to the professions has changed, and there is a less deferential acceptance of professional status and expert authority. But this change is particularly profound in architecture, where the relationship of client/user/funder – which was always complicated – has become increasingly convoluted, and where the client–architect relationship is increasingly mediated and filtered through a project manager or through the building contractor. These are people with a different agenda, which does not necessarily include high-quality architecture as the top priority.

There have been changes too in British cities and the way we inhabit them – in Manchester in particular. Increasingly we are building high and, of necessity, living in higher-density settings.

Hodder and Partners, like all architectural firms, has had to find a way to navigate this changing course of architectural practice. This book is the story of one partnership and its founder, but it is also a story about the profoundly changing nature of architectural practice at the end of the 20th century and the start of the 21st, and the story of the architecture of a post-industrial country and the particular city of Manchester. Stephen Hodder has not only experienced these changes – he has also, as practitioner, educator and RIBA President, initiated and driven them.

There is an inevitable tension between architecture as a business and architecture as an artistic pursuit. It is said that the three things needed for good architecture are time, time and time – but time is money, and that creates a fundamental conflict. Architects who do good work create the time to do this by successfully reconciling critical practice and commercial management.

So to what extent has Hodder and Partners succeeded in the pursuit of critical practice? Although it is an artificial exercise to uncouple what you do from how you do it – to disconnect the architect from the architecture – that part of the story is best told by reference to the work: the buildings. And that is the story told elsewhere in this book.

And there is of course no conclusion; no pulling together of architect and architecture to tie up a contained, neat narrative. That would be impossible to do well and too easy to do badly. The contexts for architecture – practice, people and places – are too complicated to treat in that way. And besides, Hodder and Partners is still very much at work.

HUGH PEARMAN

THE JACOBSEN INFLUENCE: FORM, TEXTURE, DETAIL AND LANDSCAPE

'You will soon find that I am a bit obsessive about my work...the vital thing is to see things grow, to start with a small sketch and see the whole and the details become reality.'
Arne Jacobsen, 1971

Arne Emil Jacobsen (1902–71) was the celebrated Danish modernist architect who designed St Catherine's College, Oxford – his only UK building. It was built in phases between 1960 and 1967. On the centenary of Jacobsen's birth, in 2002, Oxford's Museum of Modern Art ran an exhibition, 'How to be Modern: Arne Jacobsen in the 21st century'. In the accompanying book of essays, you will find one by Stephen Hodder, evaluating the Jacobsen legacy and his architecture for the college. 'Above all it brings a material world into harmony with human life', he wrote. Jacobsen's outlook and methods had informed Hodder's architectural thinking long before he won what was to be the pivotal commission of his career, and persisted through the buildings that followed in a continuing homage.

He was the architect chosen in 1992 to design the first expansion of St Catherine's, which until that point had generally been regarded as complete in itself. But no college is ever complete. Student numbers rise, needs change. The pressing need here was for more student study-bedrooms, music rehearsal rooms and (a sign of changing technology, though still in the pre-laptop, pre-internet era) computer rooms. At the time his appointment was wholly unexpected. The College had invited a number of well-regarded younger practices, all London-based and fiercely competitive, to submit ideas. None of them was aware that the retired founding Master of the College, Alan Bullock, and the younger college officials had noticed another promising-looking architect's work in a Sunday newspaper, gone to see it, and had invited him late in the day to also submit. This was Hodder, and history was repeating itself. Fishing outside the usual London pool of talent was precisely what Bullock and his then colleagues had done back in 1959 when Jacobsen himself was called in, so wrongfooting the entire British architectural establishment at a time when it was vanishingly rare for an overseas architect to win a commission in the UK.

Back then, one building had swung it for Bullock and his committee: Jacobsen's recently completed Munkegaard School in Vangede, arranged on a grid of mini-courtyards with classrooms built like tiny houses of pale yellow brick, concrete and large areas of glass. Bullock later gave one reason why Jacobsen's school had so impressed them: 'He was so sensitive to the fact that he was buEater, this clarity of design was one of the lessons Hodder learned at first hand and applied to his own projects.

Jacobsen deployed another technique which he shared with Wright: to work in private for a long time on a project which could then be produced, seemingly perfect, as if by magic. Having accepted the St Catherine's job, it was six months before he returned, and Bullock and colleagues met him at Heathrow. He had a model with him, which they insisted on unpacking there and then, in customs. There was the new St Catherine's College. 'He got it right first time', Bullock remembered. 'We only changed the position of the Master's house, because I didn't want to be near the students that lived here!' There were some similarities with Munkegaard, not least the materials – yellow brick, concrete and glass – and the grid plan, but it also owed a debt to Jacobsen's hero Mies van der Rohe, in particular his design of the considerably larger Illinois Institute of Technology campus in Chicago.

Architectural historian Nikolaus Pevsner saw it as 'the perfect piece of architecture'. So for the first expansion of the college since the feted Jacobsen original, to whom should the college look? Hodder,

Jacobsen's Munkegaard School, Vangede, north of Copenhagen, 1957

to Jacobsen's hero Mies van der Rohe, in particular his design of the considerably larger Illinois Institute of Technology campus in Chicago.

Architectural historian Nikolaus Pevsner saw it as 'the perfect piece of architecture'. So for the first expansion of the college since the feted Jacobsen original, to whom should the college look? Hodder, unlike the older, established Jacobsen, was at the outset of his career and had much less to show when commissioned – not even a school, and certainly no college. The clincher – his Munkegaard moment – was his little 1992 public swimming pool in Colne, Lancashire.

This was Hodder's first design to come to national public attention, and it was something of a younger man's show-off building, consisting of a series of angled sawtooth roofs improbably but ingeniously leaning backwards from a mast rising from the ground in front of it, thanks to the structural engineering elan of Tony Hunt, Stephen Morley and Les Postawa. Built in the depths of a severe economic recession for just £1.6m, it was an inventive response to the topography and character of the town, it maximised the use of daylight, and it worked at human scale in feel and sound and visual connection. Sports buildings tended to be introverted: not this one, with its glazed street frontage. Moreover, it had jointly won a high-profile Building of the Year award run by the Royal Fine Art Commission (RFAC) with *The Sunday Times*. The other joint winner was none other than Norman Foster's firm for the Sackler Galleries at the Royal Academy of Arts.

Foster was a hero to architects of Hodder's generation. In 1979, while studying architecture at Manchester, Hodder made a pilgrimage to the radical cultural hangar of the Sainsbury Centre for Visual Arts at the University of East Anglia, then brand new. Seeing this was a moment of epiphany, and Hodder noted the seamless engineering collaboration with Tony Hunt there. The pursuit of the finely detailed shed became an obsession for a while, though in Hodder's case for industrial clients in the north-west of England while working in the Preston office of the large multidisciplinary practice Building Design Partnership (BDP).

That was only one influence, however. Until that Fosterian revelation at East Anglia, Hodder had been immersed in the world of neo-vernacular architecture and early Frank Lloyd Wright, notably Wright's 'Prairie Style' Robie House of 1908 in Chicago. The idea of craft and technology combining would resurface when Hodder came to know Jacobsen's work – because Jacobsen, like Wright, was a total designer, producing everything right down to chairs, light fittings and door handles. Another student study visit Hodder made in 1979 was, perhaps inevitably, to St Catherine's: his tutors had referred him to the PhD thesis on Jacobsen by Rod Hackney, who had himself worked with the Danish master. This, combined with the attention to detail and a Scandi-modern sensibility communicated by his Manchester teachers such as Peter Aldington, all added up to a training in what Colin St John Wilson called 'the alternative tradition' of modernism – by which he meant an alternative to the hard-edged International Style. At the time, some of the new buildings of Manchester University itself were unorthodox in this way. You can track various influences in Hodder's work over the years, as you can with most architects – and of course the buildings of the practice reflect not just him, but his staff, who bring their own experiences to the table. The Colne pool, for all its high-tech yearnings, was in the tradition of alternative modernism, which is where I believe Hodder feels most comfortable.

Foster Associates'
Sainsbury Centre for the Visual Arts,
University of East Anglia, 1978

Come 1992 I was the architecture critic of *The Sunday Times*. I was of the same generation as Hodder, and had first come across him a decade previously when I too had worked at BDP, in my case in the London office. In the interim Hodder had set up his own practice, and at the start of that year he got in touch, as soon as he had a decent building of his own to show. I therefore went to Colne, which was not the kind of place architecture critics normally frequented back then – no less an authority than Pevsner had been somewhat dismissive of this industrial Lancashire hill town in his *Buildings of England* series. At the foot of the hill there, by the railway station, was Hodder's pool – clearly a place of ambition that was distinctly different in its broken forms, use of daylight and celebration of the town's topographical roofiness. I gave it a good *Sunday Times* write-up on 16 February 1992. 'This is a building of some sophistication, with an attention to detail that is unusual… the result is a building of palpable quality that is a credit to the town', I wrote, noting that it was a competition win built for much the same money as a basic shed.

Pendle Leisure Centre, as it is known, still looks very presentable today. The reason I seized on it at the time was because it suggested that a stylistic corner was being turned. This was budget expressive modernism coming not only in economically challenging times but also at the tail end of the tricksy postmodern period which it pointedly ignored. It had a strong sense of context – not only of the stone and slate buildings of hilly Lancashire, but also of the crinkly tin of the basic existing Nicholas Grimshaw sports hall to which the pool building was added. It is now to be found in the latest edition of *The Buildings of England* ('designed to evoke the characteristic roofscape of the town', it says, while somehow failing to note that its conjoined neighbour is by Grimshaw).

Colne Swimming Pool
from railway tracks

When it came to the Royal Fine Art Commission/ Sunday Times Building of the Year award for Colne Swimming Pool later that year, it was an older, much wiser judge who carried the day: Sir Philip Powell, joint founder of the notable postwar practice Powell and Moya. Another link, another influence: Powell and Moya's mid-1960s Cripps Building at St John's College, Cambridge, is one of the great Oxbridge buildings of the time, on a par with Catz. It too was a later influence on Hodder, most notably his St Clare's, Oxford additions of 2015–16.

This high-profile award for Colne put the firm on the map, and Hodder – his work up to that point confined to his native Lancashire – received the call, out of the blue, from Oxford. This was a challenge of quite a different order: first he had to learn how the university and this college in particular ticked, then he faced the terrifying prospect of being the first architect to add to the 'perfect' composition of Jacobsen. I remember an occasion when we met at the Institute of Contemporary Arts cafe in London, and in confidence he showed me his concept sketches. His three visually floating staircase pavilions of student rooms, perched on a perimeter wall that extended Jacobsen's precisely ordered landscape, reconciled the two grids he inherited – that of the original college, and that of the Holywell Mill Stream, a backwater of the River Cherwell running along the western boundary of the site. Both were incorporated into the geometry of the new buildings, which also picked up on the formal, proportional and material language of Jacobsen. The result was – is – a kind of hybrid architecture, a more oblique English homage to the formal Danish original. I was impressed, though I wondered if this was perhaps a slightly over-thought response. Did the buildings try to do a bit too much,

West-facing study bedrooms looking over the Holywell Mill stream at St Catherine's College, Oxford, Phase I

geometrically? But then consider what this job meant to an architect at that stage of his career. Who wouldn't burn the midnight oil, consider every detail, for something like that?

Well, we know what happened next. Hodder, the ultimate dark horse in that selection process, duly won and the architectural salons of London were all a-twitter. He had done it by going back to the mother lode – the architecture of Jacobsen – studying it and the site most carefully, and proceeding accordingly. In comparison, some of the other entries had played far more fast and loose. Perhaps that kind of essentially late-1950s modernism, with Jacobsen himself heavily in debt to the orthogonal rigour of Mies van der Rohe, was seen by some as fair game, ripe for a kicking. But what Hodder had done was to read the situation better. First, he realised the immense pride of the College's founders and their successors in their original building, and second, he anticipated the rehabilitation of mid-century modernism; something that now seems obvious but wasn't at all back then, with postmodernism still a force to be reckoned with. In a way Hodder's design helped to precipitate that rehabilitation. Even before work began on the new extension (and doubtless prompted by the prospect), in 1993 St Catherine's College was designated a Grade I-listed building. This constituted vital official recognition of the architecture of that period. Hodder found himself dealing with English Heritage as well as all the other vested and unvested interests in what was a supremely sensitive project. Working in Oxford's green belt made things still more complicated.

By 2002 – Jacobsen's centenary – the Hodder practice was firmly established. The first phase of St Catherine's had been completed, the second phase, including a new porters' lodge, was about to be

St Catherine's College, Oxford, Phase I

commissioned, the firm was dealing with sometimes difficult London projects, and in the meantime it had picked up the inaugural Stirling Prize for Architecture in 1996 for an utterly different university intervention – the Centenary Building at the University of Salford. In that building Hodder seems more relaxed. There was no heavy weight of expectation, no built-heritage constraints, no masterpiece next door. Jacobsen remained the touchstone for him, however, programmatically and at detail level. Crosswall construction, studios arranged around staircases rather than along corridors, the clear articulation of materials and details: the three-dimensional reference library of Jacobsen's Catz is used to good effect at the Centenary Building. This may not be so apparent in the dramatic external shots of the curving, almost kinetic frontage, but it comes through strongly in the carefully detailed composition of the rear and end elevations.

The alternative, humanist tradition of modern architecture as practised by Jacobsen and absorbed by Hodder goes right back to the start of the modern movement – no *tabula rasa*, more a way of designing that acknowledges history – especially in the form of the plain and simple buildings of the agricultural, vernacular tradition. Jacobsen was always keen on unselfconscious, timeless, well-made village buildings, and tried not to over-intellectualise his architecture. Hodder responded to the fact that Jacobsen preferred to trust his instincts and his sense of history rather than excessively analyse what he did. The human body – how it worked and moved and responded – was the determinant of everything for Jacobsen. His own architecture, in common with that of many of his generation, had shifted in the postwar years from his more organic 1930s 'white-modern' phase to the spare elegance and restraint of Mies.

East elevation, Centenary Building, University of Salford

Right:
Layered South elevation, Centenary Building, University of Salford

This was most notable in his slab-and-podium SAS Hotel tower in Copenhagen of 1956. In this way, Chicago came to Oxford along with Copenhagen. But Jacobsen was always much more than an imitator of the great German-American architect: he brought that Scandinavian humanity to the project, and this resonated with Hodder.

Hodder is not a manifesto-writing architect but he saw one in the essence of Jacobsen's approach: 'The continuity of tradition and culture, suffused with innate considerations of proportion, colour, materiality and texture, together with concerns for how things are made and their legibility, were ingrained in Jacobsen and represent a contemporary and timeless architectural manifesto', he wrote in his centenary appreciation. This, then, is the framework in which to consider the buildings of the Hodder practice, obviously at Catz but also elsewhere.

Catz was to be the start of a career-defining relationship between architect and client which – at the time of writing – is now in its 25th year. A lot of that time has been spent in building new – the second phase of student rooms there, arranged in an L-shaped configuration completing the original perimeter plan, are simpler and more confident. The Jacobsen architectural and landscape language lessons have been thoroughly learned. But there has been another kind of work: acting as steward to the original Jacobsen buildings, supervising conservation and upgrade work. This might not be immediately apparent – replacement solar-control windows, for instance, are not a glamorous thing. But on the other hand they are absolutely vital to the character of the original architecture, as anyone who weeps at the sight of a good building given inappropriate replacement windows well knows. Here the task

Jacobsen's SAS Royal Hotel,
Copenhagen, 1956

SAS
RESTAURANT

was at least partly to put right problems caused by the 'value engineering' of the original building: for instance, Jacobsen had designed sunshading louvres which were omitted when it was built. And it faces west, with large areas of glass: go figure. Such work might not feature prominently in the magazines but – working with the Jacobsen Foundation and with the successor practice, Dissing+Weitling – it is well done.

To gain an insight into the way Jacobsen worked, I met with Peter Denney, a British architect who joined his office in Copenhagen in 1962. 'The moment I got there, I was working on St Catherine's. It was a going project, progressing on site', he said. When Jacobsen's project architect Knud Holscher left after the first phase, Denney stepped up and became closely involved in finishing off what was by then an enlarged design, doing all the development drawings. When the go-ahead came for building to recommence, Denney returned to England, and to Oxford. He was there from 1965 to 1967, finishing the College and its landscape. Jacobsen would drop by two or three times a year ('It was like a Danish home from home – he'd take us out to tea at the Mitre') and Denney would talk to him on the phone most days.

'He was a master at working *through* people – it was almost osmotic', he says. Jacobsen would gather around him the necessary practitioners – in architecture, furniture design, lighting, whatever – and gently but firmly get his concepts across, relying on them to act as his eyes and ears when it came to detail and quality. He didn't always win – the bricks at Catz, though yellow like Munkegaard, were of lesser quality. This was a new Oxford college with none of the accumulated wealth of the ancient foundations. Nonetheless the laying of the brick courses was precisely determined. The 'perpends' – the vertical

Conversion of the former Porters' Lodge to teaching accommodation joints – had to line up perfectly. You can still see some pencil marks where the builders dutifully spaced them exactly. This attention to detail was something that Hodder (himself a stickler for detail) noted about the College – along with such details as the perfect shadow gaps, and subtle, sometimes adventurous use of glazing. Famously the deep, slender, smooth concrete beams of the dining hall roof are made to 'float' by piercing the high-level clerestory glazing. This is a masterly touch, which also helps generate the clever rhythmic articulation of the brick-box exterior of the dining hall. And as Holscher later recounted, when it came to the precast concrete elements such as those beams at St Catherine's, only perfection would do: 'The concrete components were checked one by one, first at the factory and then on their arrival in Oxford – the slightest scratch and a new one had to be made.' Jacobsen, whose first training before architecture was as a stonemason, and who personally demonstrated to the builders how to make the brickwork his way, was not going to be fobbed off with inferior workmanship.

You might imagine that Denney would feel proprietorial about the college he helped design in his youth, and fiercely protective of it and the reputation of Jacobsen. And of course he is, but he also believes in progress. Consequently he is generous in his praise for Hodder's northerly extensions to the College, and for his role as the college's architect in working with him and with Dissing+Weitling in sensitively upgrading the original buildings, part-funded by the Jacobsen Foundation. Talking of the last part of the job he originally built there – the little punt house and caretaker's house on the Holywell Mill Stream – Denney notes approvingly how Hodder's buildings have advanced to meet and embrace it. 'He did that very well, very cleverly', he says. 'And Stephen's got better bricks.'

Articulated concrete structure,
St Catherine's College dining hall

St Catherine's College, Oxford,
Phase II

Just as Jacobsen took the trouble to examine the layouts of traditional Oxford colleges before drawing a line – and adopted the traditional rooms-around-a-staircase, buildings-around-a-quad approach, even if it did look radically different from its predecessors – so Hodder in turn took pains to immerse himself in the architectural language of Jacobsen. This ranges from the basic forms, proportions and materials of the buildings through to the very architectural landscape of walls, rails and yew hedges that Jacobsen instigated – all set to a precise two-metre height, with walls becoming hedges and vice versa. This regular, rectilinear organisation of the landscape is a language that Hodder faithfully replicated as he expanded the footprint of the college northwards. Now that the new landscape there has matured, it is notable how effective these ingredients have proved to be in Hodder's hands when, for instance, he came to tackle the area of car parking between his first and second phases of new buildings. Instead of being a quad, it is a sequence of architectural spaces using the language of the original in a new way.

What is equally apparent is how deftly the new buildings flip the axis of the original composition, so that the western edge of the Jacobsen enfilade, continued north as an imaginary line, becomes the eastern edge of the second phase of Hodder buildings. It will be interesting to see how any future expansion of the college on the remaining north-east corner of the site – all that's left, overlooking meadows and sports fields – manages to preserve the setting of the original. There is no doubt it will survive. As Denney says, when discussing the various carefully designed alterations and upgrades so far: 'It's got colossal character. It's still a Jacobsen building.'

First floor gallery,
Arumugam Building,
St Catherine's College, Oxford,
Phase II

Staircase,
Arumugam Building,
St Catherine's College, Oxford,
Phase II

Of Hodder's initial design response right back in the early 1990s, Denny remarks: 'I thought it was brilliant, and still do. The other schemes were so cavalier in their attitudes to the original buildings. I think Stephen's was the only one that showed proper understanding of what it was about.'

Since then, his involvement with Catz has amounted to a second architectural education for Hodder. Jacobsen's sparing choice of materials, his skilful interweaving of traditionalism and modernism and of buildings with landscape, and his eye for the telling detail and the separation of forms are key here. So is the interaction with Jacobsen's surviving colleagues and the Foundation. All this has fed through into the work of the Hodder practice and inevitably informed its projects elsewhere. I'd point to the manner in which he now uses precast concrete components or timber to make certain urban buildings, for instance, and the way he sits others into existing landscapes, such as the National Wildflower Centre at Knowsley (now sadly abandoned) or the new visitor centre to be built for the Royal Horticultural Society Garden Bridgewater – the RHS's fifth – in Worsley.

Sometimes the influence is less obvious, but once you get used to the Jacobsen language of clarity, articulation, materiality and telling detail you find it glimmering away, as discussed at Salford University's Centenary Building. You might, for instance, look to St Clare's in Oxford, completed in 2015, where the precedent of Powell and Moya in Cambridge is acknowledged in timber rather than concrete – but where the design of the corridors, with a strip of light set directly just above each of the study-bedroom doors, is a straight homage to the master's SAS Hotel in Copenhagen. The Warden's House there also directly references Catz.

South residential pavilion,
St Clare's, Oxford

Left:
Warden's Lodge,
St Clare's, Oxford

Overleaf:
Corridor, garden pavilion,
St Clare's, Oxford

Also there is the 1998 Careers Service Unit for Manchester University, which is somewhat Corbusian in feel but is defined by a plinth wall in precast concrete based on the two-metre wall-hedge height that works so well at Catz, topped with a characteristic glazed clerestory. Jacobsen was adept at proportioning, probably using a version of the golden section to make his buildings human scale. Le Corbusier, of course, had his equivalent, the Modulor. Here Hodder very legibly combines his influences and in many buildings deploys the Jacobsen trick of visually sliding the component masses of his buildings past each other. You see this working horizontally at the Centenary Building in Salford and at the CSU, and vertically at the 2012 Great Marlborough Street 'Student Castle' tower in Manchester, which is a bundle of slender sections of differing heights laid and slid against each other. Nearly always the proportions of Hodder's windows and cladding modules can be traced back to Jacobsen.

Careers Service Unit,
University of Manchester

Great Marlborough Street rising
from Manchester's skyline

Right:
Great Marlborough Street at the
junction of New Wakefield Street

Great Marlborough Street, juxtaposed with Sir Alfred Waterhouse's former Refuge Assurance building (now the Principal Hotel)

Elsewhere an industrial aesthetic is refined (that Jacobsen articulation and separation of forms, and use of shadow gaps), for instance at the 55 Princess Street office building of 2006 in Manchester. By delineating and shuffling the masses – projecting here, receding there – the bulk of the building is tamed, responding to the great Town Hall opposite. Even in an early adaptive project, Manchester's CUBE gallery from 1998, Hodder borrows a Jacobsen detail from Catz: the way the staircase meets the ground via an intermediate plinth coming up to meet it. And although the Dane never did anything like Hodder's 'hyperbolic paraboloid' Corporation Street Footbridge of 1999, also in Manchester, again you see the clear articulation of the parts – taut glass skin, steel cable structure, floating walkway/ramp – that makes you appreciate the building as a precise assemblage. You see how it works, how it all came together, and why. It's more than a 'kit of parts' approach, it is a sophisticated way of dealing with mass, light and the sensation of weight and movement and textures.

Architects always like to cite their influences and inspirations, and Hodder is very clear where his lie. This is a profession, an art and a science in which there is a historic continuum. No good idea is ever wasted, though it can be adapted and developed. For Hodder and his practice, the encounter over many years with the work of one of the great modern masters at the peak of his powers has been overwhelmingly positive, and has fed through to become an almost instinctive language of design. So much was to stem from that phone call from Oxford in 1992. The Jacobsen project continues, in other buildings and other places.

Interior, CUBE gallery

Right:
55 Princess Street, Manchester,
sitting astride two conservation areas

Aurora
56,476 SQ FT
GRADE 'A' OFFICES
21 CAR SPACES
TO LET
6,202 SQFT
9,030 SQFT
Debenham Tie Leung
TO LET
HIGH QUALITY
SELF CONTAINED
OFFICE
ACCOMMODATION
122 SQM
(1,316 SQFT)

The 'hyperbolic paraboloid' of
Corporation Street footbridge

TONY
CHAPMAN

SPIRIT OF PLACE: LATENT QUALITIES IN ARCHITECTURE

'The spaces where life occurs are places... A place is a space which has a distinct character... Architecture means to visualize the genius loci and the task of the architect is to create meaningful places, whereby he helps man to dwell.'
Christian Norberg-Schulz, *Genius Loci*, 1980

St Paul's Place, Sheffield, an office building within the Heart of the City Masterplan

Architects are collectors; they find their inspiration everywhere, gleaning ideas where they may. Sometimes this comes from their reading or their conversations, sometimes from their education and their experience, but often from their travels – and not only from going to see buildings by people they admire, or ones they don't know well – they also find it in place, and in the atmospheres that belong to places. Sometimes these atmospheres have been conjured by another architect, but often they are inherent.

For example Sheffield has one atmosphere, Manchester a quite different one – it's in the air. Good buildings help, of course, and the spaces between them, but an atmosphere is not always planned. Bad architecture can definitely damage the spirit of a place. Good architects design buildings that generate a spirit – or at least enhance the spirit that already exists in a locale.

The writer Lawrence Durrell was no lover of modern architecture. Along with many 20th century intellectuals, and various others, he thought that the impact of new building was generally negative. In a BBC TV documentary about Greece he made in 1976 called *Spirit of Place*, he said: 'The important determinant of any culture is the spirit of place... a country will always bear the unmistakable signature of the place... We've seen it spoilt, we've sacrificed a great deal on the cultural side, but there has never been a culture so enormously rich in its matter; the mystery is why it's so ugly. Because we have at our disposal five thousand times more than Solomon ever had to build a temple with, but where the hell is our architecture coming from?... Because it's only an exteriorisation of what you feel – the minute you start drawing you are uncoiling the contents of your subconscious.' This might well help to explain some architecture.

William Morris thought much the same of most 19th century architecture. In his very first public lecture, delivered before the Trades Guild of Learning in 1878 and entitled *The Lesser Arts*, he said: 'A great uprising of ecclesiastical zeal, coinciding with the great increase of study, and consequently of knowledge of medieval architecture, has driven people into spending their money on these buildings, not merely with the purpose of repairing them, keeping them safe, clean, and wind- and water-tight, but also of "restoring" them to some ideal state of perfection; sweeping away if possible all signs of what has befallen them at least since the Reformation … To deal recklessly with valuable (and national) monuments which, when once gone, can never be replaced by any splendour of modern Art, is doing very sorry service to the State.'

Peter Zumthor is another man who is deeply sensitive to the atmosphere of place. In 2006 he published *Atmospheres*, in which he wrote: 'How do people design things with such a beautiful natural presence, things that move me every single time? One word for it is atmosphere.' And in his Royal Gold Medal lecture in 2013 he said: 'If it's possible to construct presence in literature, maybe it is possible to construct presence in architecture, something so silent and self-evident, needing no commentary, something that should be and not mean.'

The Romans spoke of the *genius loci* – specifically the deity who guarded a place – but in more general terms it refers to the spirit or soul of a place.

Respect for this spirit does not mean that we should venerate the old for its own sake; still less that we should build pastiche. But it does mean architects should take care to listen to what a site is saying to them. Sometimes the architect creates

Motel One, Manchester

Overleaf:
St Catherine's College, Oxford, showing Jacobsen's bell tower

a building's spirit from scratch, sometimes it is already in residence. At St Catherine's, Oxford, Stephen Hodder inherited the spirit of Arne Jacobsen, though modernism and Oxford have never been natural bedfellows. The university had flirted with Maxwell Fry in the late 1930s (though his designs for All Soul's were never built), before appointing Architects' Co-Partnership at St John's in 1960, and taking a much riskier plunge with James Stirling's Florey Building in the early 1970s. Jacobsen was chosen by the enlightened client, historian Alan Bullock, over the likes of Powell and Moya, Richard Sheppard, YRM and ACP, and the attraction between Jacobsen and St Catherine's was immediate and productive. The resulting building has been lovingly cared for by a dedicated management team, and so looks as good now as it did the day it opened.

Twenty of the 25 years that Hodder has run his own practice have been spent at St Catherine's, so there has been no more important project for him. For a man schooled in Manchester in the tradition of the Scandinavian modernists it was the perfect commission, and one he never dreamed might come his way so quickly when just a few years qualified. Modernism was at a crossroads: one way lay Jacobsen and Leslie Martin, the other path was that taken by Archigram and Richard Rogers, and patrolling the junction was Norman Foster, another alumnus of Manchester. But the Manchester School of Architecture also has another strong tradition in that it teaches the importance of craft, of making and of the way in which people use buildings, and those two threads run through all Hodder's buildings.

The process of Hodder's appointment was very similar to that of Jacobsen: a committee went to look at some buildings and decided whether or not they

St Catherine's College, Oxford,
Phase II from the water garden

wanted the architect to do their building – it's the Oxford way, patronage in a positive sense. Most young architects would have been awed by the prospect of building on the site of a master, but not Hodder. Nor was he content simply to follow in Jacobsen's footsteps. For Hodder context is about responsiveness, and he works best where there is a strong context to react to. So, as has always been his wont, he spent time on site searching for and imbibing the spirit of the place – Oxford as well as St Catherine's – trying to uncover its mystery, its latent qualities as he calls them, and finding out what it is about a place that can give rise to an idea. With St Catherine's there is a very obvious reinterpretation of what is already there. An Oxford college provides the precedent of study-bedrooms arranged around a staircase, and this is a strong generator of ideas. But for Hodder making places is also about creating a sense of belonging; about creating places that can be occupied by people.

Jacobsen's was a very hard act to follow. The College may no longer be able to afford the brass door furniture, and the concrete may not have quite the same buttery quality – 'shuttered with Lurpak', as has been said – but the detailing is just as fine, the architecture as considered. Hodder restored Jacobsen's Junior Common Room, floated a monocoque roof over what was a courtyard, and created a new lecture theatre (assumed by many to be Jacobsen's). Otherwise, apart from replacing some glazing, he left well alone.

The new work, in two phases (1995 and 2006), is respectful but by no means slavish. Hodder noted the inward-looking nature of Jacobsen's work and, still in keeping with the collegiate approach, turned it inside out. Phase I addresses the river and the city: the setting is bucolic, the architecture urbane. The scheme looks deliberately outwards, creating a place where people can sit and dwell. At one point elements

St Catherine's College, Oxford, Phase I

of the wall fragment and form little seats next to the river, encouraging people to populate the place – because Hodder knows well that people make places.

In Phase I Hodder took Jacobsen's three-metre grid and used it to link the new accommodation – 54 study-bedrooms – to that occupied by the students living within the original college walls. Inside, the rooms are more generous than Jacobsen's and better appointed, with the en-suite facilities demanded by the conference market (as well as today's students). The all-important staircases, equally, are outward-looking, letting light in rather than being enclosed.

Phase II completes the plan (save for a further extension to accommodate the Middle Common Room and more postgrad rooms) with 132 more study-bedrooms in seven pavilions, plus four seminar rooms, and it gives the College the entrance it lacked. It speaks the same language as Phase I. It was also delivered through design and build – a procurement system that seldom produces work as good as this.

Like artists and planners, architects talk about positive and negative space. For artists and architects negative space is the space between the objects and the buildings; for planners, in the eyes of architects at least, it's called the space left over after planning (SLOAP). Good architects make a positive out of the negative, and at St Catherine's the spirit of the place is not just about creating negative space that people can occupy, between the Jacobsen scheme and the river, it also resides in the buildings themselves: in Hodder's responsiveness to the materiality of the original, and to Jacobsen's three-metre module and the grid this generated.

Elsewhere in Oxford, as part of Rick Mather's masterplan for the disparate St Clare's (2015) around Banbury Road, Hodder created a quadrangle of pavilions abutting and behind the late Arts and

Staircase 17,
St Catherine's College, Oxford,
Phase I

Crafts house by Henry T. Hare – like Hodder, a former President of the RIBA, albeit a century earlier. St Clare's is not a college of the University of Oxford; rather it is an international college for 16–18-year-olds whose parents hope some of the magic of the more venerable Oxford institution might rub off on their offspring.

The new work reacts to its context in terms of both the locale and the city; to the house and to the collegiate architecture of Oxford. It turns what was an ordinary garden into a very Oxford place: a quadrangle composed of the rear of the old house, two narrow-plan pavilions that hinge off it, and a third facing the house comprising two elements linked by a glazed bridge. Overall the five new buildings provide 36 study-bedrooms, rooms for three wardens, two common rooms and an art studio. Materially the buildings are very un-Oxford, being of timber, with exposed structural cross-laminated timber (CLT) used in the art wing to allow a cantilever over an old wall that produces more accommodation and more light. The 100mm-thick CLT walls of the residential pavilions are clad in oak to reflect the original building. The richness of wood lends a very different, more intimate quality to the place.

There are 70 students living at St Clare's, and Hodder was seeking a device that would hold them together as a community and provide a common space that they could inhabit. He believed the historic notion of the quadrangle would do just that. This was not part of the brief, but the client was wise enough to recognise and go with an architectural idea based on the precedents set by the university. Architect and client shared a belief that these students were worthy of architecture every bit as good as that afforded to students of the university. The scheme borrows other

The garden cloister, St Clare's, Oxford

elements from collegiate design in the staircase and the cloister that shelters the art room. These enhance the sense of place and belonging for the inhabitants.

In another quarter of Oxford Hodder has built a very different scheme, St Clement's (2011), since renamed Alice House. Though again not an Oxford college, it does provide postgraduate accommodation for the university. And, as at St Catherine's, there is a strong architectural context, here provided by the brutalism of James Stirling's neighbouring Florey Building. Unlike at St Catherine's, Hodder chose to react to rather than empathise with the older architecture, creating a gentle, tactile scheme that spans the recreated Penson's Gardens with a delicately glazed bridge and presents well-modulated facades to the Angel and Greyhound water meadows, as well as dealing with the fine urban grain of St Clement's Street. Instead of defining the place, this scheme is made by the place – a place previously made by James Stirling. Within the horseshoe plan there is the pragmatic provision of 140 studios and 80 public car parking spaces. There is a strongly expressed concrete frame with an infill of creamy brick, with windows angled to admit light from two sides.

Hodder's most lauded academic commission could scarcely have been more different from St Catherine's. The University of Oxford is the oldest university in the English-speaking world, founded in 1167; the University of Salford was founded exactly 800 years later as the Royal Technical Institute, Salford, acquiring full university status in 1967. An alumnus of the predecessor college, the Royal Technical Institute, Salford, was the painter L.S. Lowry. Although born across the border in Stretford, the artist has long been associated with Salford, and his work has in many

Alice House, Oxford, post-graduate accommodation, St Clements, Oxford

Right:
The interior 'street', Centenary Building, University of Salford

ways defined the spirit of the city. Lowry's *A View from the Window of the Royal Technical College, Salford* (1924) was drawn from an upper-floor window. His work is hung and celebrated at The Lowry, Michael Wilford's gallery and theatre, which has done much to enhance the cultural and intellectual reputation of the city.

The aim of the commission for the Centenary Building, part of the Adelphi Campus, was to attempt a similar thing, and to change Salford's reputation (as seen from Manchester) as something of a wilderness.

The appointment of Hodder – still young, still making his way – meant the university had an architect who was willing to work swiftly and to be flexible. This was just as well, as the brief changed entirely during the short gestation of the job to accommodate the Departments of Interior Architecture, Design Studies, Graphic and Industrial Design, containing a total of 400 students.

Hodder's plan, derived in part from St Catherine's, provides three layers of accommodation: the first, four-storey layer, an orthogonal strip facing eastwards towards the town, provides simple rectangular studios and seminar rooms; this is separated by the top-lit internal street from the second layer, a three-storey strip of cellular rooms for tutors; then a third layer faces inwards towards the rest of the college, accommodating CAD suites, lecture theatres and studios.

Internally the building has a very special quality: the tall, narrow internal street is dynamic; top light washes down one side and is complemented by artificial light. It is not too fanciful to see in the creation of the street the transposition of the natural animation of the street life of a city-centre university such as Manchester or Oxford to a bleak edge-of-town campus.

L.S. Lowry *A View from the Window of Royal Technical College, Salford, Looking Towards Manchester* 1924
© The Lowry Collection, Salford

Left:
North elevation, Centenary Building, University of Salford

For Hodder the Centenary Building, which won the first Stirling Prize in 1996, was about the abstraction of a context between the city and the university, sitting as it does astride that edge between the two. The solution arose out of a search to uncover the mystery of place; its latent qualities. What is it, he asks himself with every project, about a place that can give rise to an idea?

So how far does the spirit of a place imbue Hodder's architecture, and how far does his architecture imbue the place? Cities have a spirit that is unique to each of them. It is part of what engenders civic pride, and it's related to the fabric of the city. If Hodder is designing a building on Market Street in Newcastle it will be a building which responds to the particular qualities of that city; if he is doing a building in Oxford then its spirit will depend on his understanding of what he believes the qualities of that city to be. And the very shape of his Ovatus towers in Liverpool depends on the unique light quality reflected off the water, and provides 360-degree views to their residents of the estuary and the city.

Manchester is a city whose pride, even its identity, took a battering from the IRA bomb of 1996. The devastation was on a different scale from anywhere else in Britain, with all the buildings within a half-mile radius of the explosion damaged. The response represents a rare example of true civic leadership. Council Leader Sir Richard Leese and Chief Executive Sir Howard Bernstein did not want to replace like-for-like; they wanted to build a better city, one that was not just about commerce but about leisure, and not in the organised sense of sporting or entertainment facilities. Rather they wanted to make places and squares for Mancunians, and called on local architects to help them achieve their vision.

Centenary Building,
University of Salford

Ovatus I and II residential towers in Liverpool, overlooking the estuary

Hodder describes his Corporation Street Footbridge (1999) as an act of defiance, though he is modest about the size of the achievement, saying that other architects and urban designers made far greater gestures in the remaking of the city. But he does recognise the significance of the bridge, not least because of its position at the epicentre of the bombing. So it is a symbolic move, but it is also a physical one – it performs the practical job of dealing with the sectional change between the two shopping centres. It is a hyperbolic paraboloid, and the boardwalk threads through it creating a symmetry with the street. From it you can look up the gentle arc of Corporation Street towards the newly civic Albert Square. And the fragility of the glass was deliberate: it seems to say 'we can do this, we will make it like this'.

The same principles apply to other less obviously civic buildings. The housing at Cambridge Street, Manchester, uses a white brick – not because this material is particularly characteristic of the city, but because it marks a key building, in the same way that Portland Stone does in inner-city structures. It also allows, within a budget, the sculpting of form which Hodder enjoys so much. The client wanted balconies, but the city is known for its unpredictable weather – the brick form allows the facades to be cut back, sheltering the balconies. Cambridge Street is defined within Terry Farrell's masterplan as a gateway, so the building does have to take its place within an urban structure. The design thinking for Cambridge Street arose directly from a rigorous testing of the place, resulting in an integrity in the architectural language.

The spirit of place is different in urban and rural settings. Inevitably it is to do with the bustle of the one and the quietude of the other (although pockets of peace can equally be created in cities). For Hodder

Corporation Street Footbridge, Manchester

Right:
No. 1 Cambridge Street, Manchester

Overleaf:
Colne Swimming Pool, Lancashire

20
YG63 NYD

DEWHU

the thinking is not dependent on the setting – rural or urban – but the architectural outcomes are inevitably different. A leisure facility such as a swimming pool is a *rus in urbe* project – it is about evoking the spirit of the country within the city, allowing the users to think they are elsewhere, on holiday perhaps, and not in one of the uncompromising urban settings typical of Hodder's pools.

One of his earliest completed buildings was Colne Swimming Pool (1992) in Lancashire. The scheme uses a plinth of local stone to tie what is a sizeable structure in a small-scale town into its setting, and to generate a sense of place. The north-light sawtooth roof evokes not only the local mills but also the way in which the mill towns themselves cascade down the Pennine foothills. The pool has been well looked after by the local authority; the same cannot be said of another of Hodder's pools: Darlaston Swimming Pool (2001) in Walsall, which has been likened to a mini-Acropolis on its bluff of rising land.

'If the roof doesn't leak, the architect hasn't been creative enough.' So said Philip Johnson of Frank Lloyd Wright, while conceding that if Wright's were 17-bucket houses, his Glass House was certainly a six-bucket job. Hodder has always been interested in building technology, and his architecture has pushed at the boundaries of art. But better that than settle for the ordinary, the easily doable. Far more worrying has been the mismanagement and poor maintenance of some of his schemes.

At Darlaston the lack of maintenance has resulted in a structure that, far from enhancing its environs as it did for many years, now does little to raise local spirits. Intended as a symbol of the planned regeneration of Darlaston, rather it symbolises the consequences of the 2008 financial crash and

Darlaston Swimming Pool, Walsall

the subsequent local authority cuts. And it shows how the management (or lack of management) of a building can affect the spirit of a whole place.

If that is true, can the spirit of a building survive decay, and even its destruction? The most poetic of Hodder's pools was perhaps Berners Pool (2003) at Grange-over-Sands in Cumbria, which used the natural fall of the site to embed the pool within its Miesian plinth. It was designed to capture the spirit of the adjacent abandoned 1930s lido, on a site overlooking Morecambe Bay. So the context was both manmade and natural. Hodder responded with a lightweight, very 21st century building that seemed consciously to have borrowed its site from nature. Which indeed it had, because this beautiful pool, one of Hodder's finest works, was destroyed in 2013 and replaced by executive housing. As with Darlaston it was a victim of the cuts: South Lakeland District Council who owned the site were unable to support the Trust when it got into difficulties – which was almost inevitable, because no local authority manages to run a pool at a profit.

The pool had been a community project from the outset, with local residents setting up a trust to raise the money, appoint the architects and oversee the build and the running of the pool. A sponsored walk raised £800,000 from 1,000 people, whose names were etched in a screen at the pool in recognition of their commitment. Matching funding was provided by Sport England. One 90-year-old gentleman, who had been a member of Grange-over-Sands swimming club from the early days of the lido, would every day lower himself from his walking frame into the new pool. He thought the quality of the swimming with its views over the bay was unsurpassed.

Berners Pool, Grange-over-Sands, Cumbria

When awarding it an RIBA Award in 2004, the judges enthused: 'Wherever you are in the building, whether in among the excitement of the pool or the mental relaxation of the gym, the eye can stray out to the calm beyond, be it the sea in front of you or the woodland to one side. Even on a damp, dull day the building creates a sense of joy.' It is not altogether fanciful on visiting the former site to sense something of the spirit of a fine building, one that post-dates it just as it pre-dated the pool.

Another Hodder project has faced similar mis-management. The National Wildflower Centre (2000) in Knowsley on Merseyside, one of the poorest boroughs in the country, closed its doors at the end of 2016. Like Berners Pool it demonstrates the short-term thinking that went into so many millennium projects. In Darlaston and Grange-over-Sands it was Sports Lottery funding that got the projects built but not properly maintained; in Knowsley it was Millennium Commission funding. Again, a trust was responsible for running the centre – Landlife, a charity that promotes botanical research and engages the public in creative conservation.

Sited in a public park on what was William Gladstone's estate and opposite his stables, the building is a literal one-liner, a monumental in-situ concrete structure 160 metres long by 4 metres deep, with a rooftop walkway that pre-dates New York's High Line Park. The 2001 RIBA Awards judges' citation read: 'What is brilliant is that the singularity of the idea does not suppress responses to the various situations which occur along its length, but is interpreted so as to create a series of surprising and beautiful episodes, startling transparencies,

National Wildflower Centre,
Knowsley

views, foliage suddenly framed, interiors engaging with landscapes and unexpected shafts of daylight and sunlight penetrating through glazed slots in the terrace above.'

In the spring of 2017, shut off from its public by heavy-duty steel fencing and razor wire, the closed Centre has taken on a new spirit – one that closely resembles Gillespie Kidd & Coia's abandoned 1960s masterpiece St Peter's Seminary, Cardross, near Glasgow: the same defiant modernism, the same sadness at its abandonment.

An uncannily similar though much larger project is set to take the place of the Wildflower Centre in the Hodder oeuvre: the latest of the UK's National Gardens at New Hall, Worsley. The site is one of the lost gardens of England, once attached to the hall designed by Edward Blore, the architect who took over the design of Buckingham Palace from John Nash, and whose own work there was largely obscured by Aston Webb. His work at Worsley was destroyed in 1949 after the hall had fallen into disrepair. The RHS appointed the landscape gardener Tom Stuart-Smith to do the landscape design and Stephen Hodder to conserve the existing buildings and design a visitor centre overlooking a new lake.

This is the culmination of a longstanding interest in architecture in a landscape for Hodder, who had been involved previously in two aborted projects. In 1995 he was invited to design a visitor centre in an extension to Heaton Hall, a Grade I-listed Palladian-style Georgian hall by James Wyatt. There he planned a sunken courtyard to get natural light into office accommodation. And in 2002 Hodder was runner-up to an unbuilt competition design by Benson & Forsyth to build and design a visitor centre-cum-exhibition space for the Beamish Open Air Museum in County

National Wildflower Centre today

Broken wall, RHS Garden Bridgewater

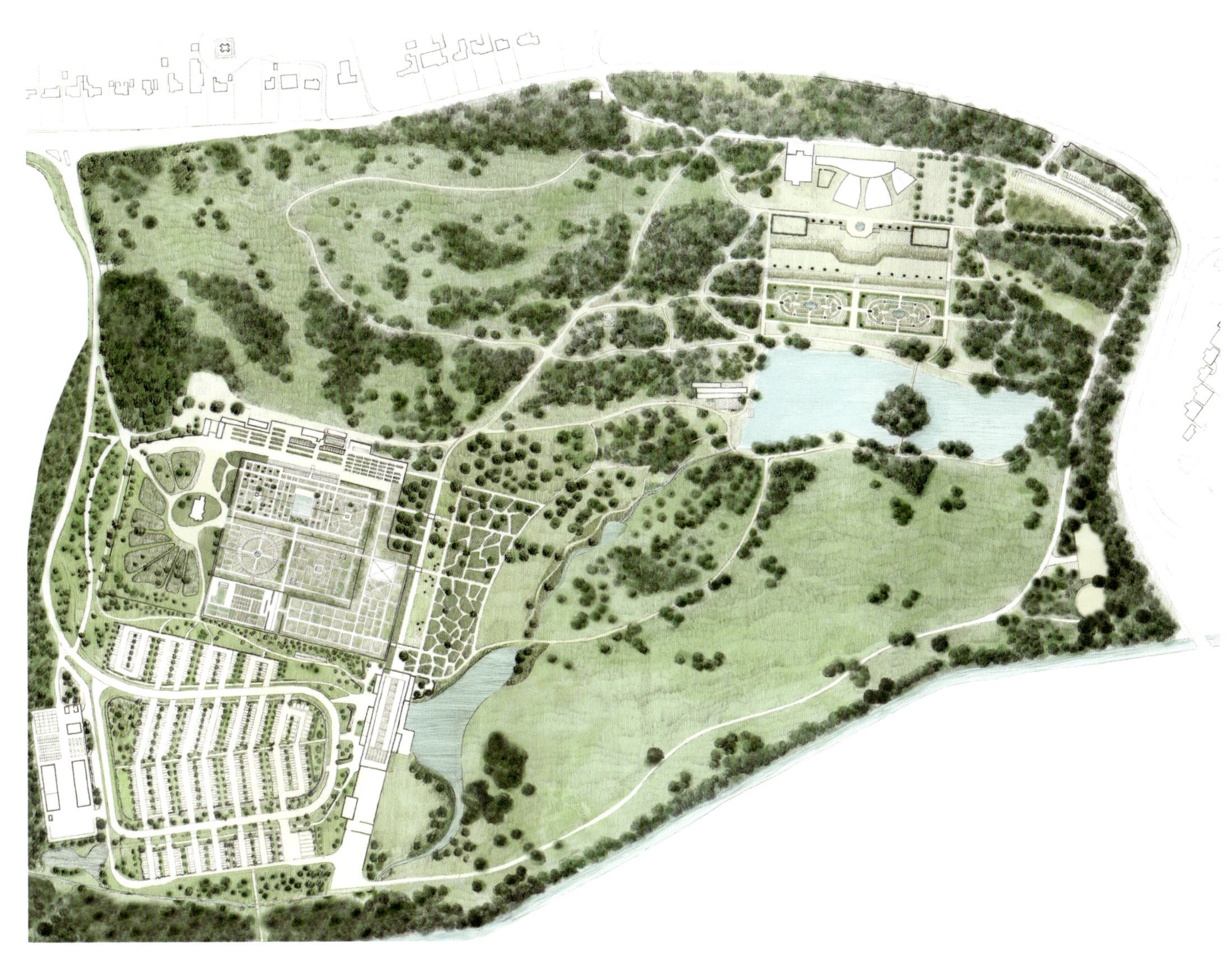

RHS Garden, Bridgewater, masterplan, Tom Stuart-Smith

Durham. Hodder's scheme was unique to its setting, with linked pavilions zigzagging across the contours and losing themselves in the landscape.

Much of this thinking was carried forward into the fifth National Garden at Worsley New Hall, named RHS Garden Bridgewater after the canal which forms the southern boundary of the site. Elsewhere along its course, the canal has defined much of the regeneration of Manchester and Salford.

The spirit of the existing place is determined largely by its dereliction; its dormancy. In the overgrown four-hectare walled kitchen garden, untended for over a decade, the vegetation is feral, the greenhouses that abut the garden walls breed weeds, and many of their panes are cracked or smashed. The potting sheds are obscurely sinister, the stables horseless.

Hodder's task is to retain some sense of the mystery and intrigue that currently pervades the place, while providing all the facilities visitors to the new National Garden require, and so levy the money the RHS needs to continue its good work. The architects will doubtless pay some heed to the statement of purpose expressed by the Society for the Protection of Ancient Buildings: 'As good buildings age, the bond with their sites strengthens. A beautiful, interesting or simply ancient building still belongs where it stands, however corrupted that place may have become. Use and adaptation of buildings leave their marks and these, in time, we also see as aspects of the building's integrity.'

There is poetry in Salford, in Darlaston and in Knowsley every bit as much as there is in Oxford, at Beamish and in Grange-over-Sands. The poetry does not begin in Stephen Hodder's head; it begins in that least poetic document, the brief, and it derives from listening to the brief, visiting the site and thinking about what is there and what might be. Therein lies Hodder's refined sense of place.

The welcome building,
RHS Garden Bridgewater

Berners Pool,
Grange-over-Sands, Cumbria
at sunset over Morecombe Bay

LAURA MARK

HODDER AND PARTNERS: A MANCHESTER PRACTICE

'For Manchester is the place where people do things... "Don't talk about what you are going to do, do it." That is the Manchester habit. And in the past through the manifestation of this quality the word Manchester became a synonym for energy and freedom and the right to do and to think without shackles.'
Judge Parry, *What The Judge Saw*, 1912

During the heady Madchester days of the 1980s and early 1990s – the years of the Happy Mondays, The Stone Roses, The Smiths, Joy Division, the Hacienda and Factory Records – Manchester was thriving. It was a hub of ingenuity, whether for music, for art, or for architecture, yet it looked significantly different from the city we see today. There were still empty warehouses and decaying buildings – a sign of the city's once-thriving cotton industry – and it was these that provided cheap rents and thus a place for creativity and resourcefulness to thrive. From this hive of activity arose a heady desire for the city to forge its own path.

It was during the mid-1990s that Stephen Hodder decided to move his small practice from Lytham, where he had set up on his own (then named Hodder Associates) after leaving Building Design Partnership (BDP), to Manchester. This signalled a change for the up-and-coming firm. It was a time when many were beginning to see the potential in Manchester as a northern second city, and an alternative to the bright lights of London. Architectural practices in Manchester were starting to make their mark with the beginnings of what would become nationally recognised regeneration projects, developers were tapping into the city's potential, and a scene of regeneration and development was emerging alongside its famous and unrivalled music scene.

For Hodder, this move to Manchester would begin a relationship which has lasted for more than 20 years, resulted in more than 60 projects – built and unbuilt – and made a lasting impact on the city. Manchester's own regeneration has intertwined with the development of this northern architectural practice.

The story really starts around a decade after Hodder's move to Manchester. The practice had begun to build up a body of well-regarded work, but this really took off with the regeneration of Hulme, to the south of Manchester city centre. Hulme's renewal would go on to become one of the UK's most important urban regeneration projects.

By the late 1990s, Hulme was already undergoing its third generation of transformation. The slum clearances of the 1960s were followed by the construction of Britain's largest system-built housing estate – known as the Hulme Crescents. However, this was soon followed by the realisation that the estate had been built too fast and was slowly rotting, blighted by poor maintenance and social problems. It was no longer a place where families wanted to live, and after a decade of deliberation Hulme's crescents of 1,000 homes were to be razed to the ground and more than 12,000 residents rehomed.

The eight-storey concrete deck-access blocks were once again replaced with the terraced streets of the past. It was within these new streets that Hodder Associates constructed a domestically scaled addition to the local community – a small doctors' surgery intended to restitch the area's blighted urban fabric and provide vital local services.

Although the whole Hulme regeneration project was itself large and unwieldly, replacing huge swathes of homes and completely changing the character of the area, the regeneration offered a chance for smaller practices to be involved through interventions such as the City Road Surgery. It was in this project, with its modest materiality and form, and using a simple palette of bricks, glazed blocks and steel, that Hodder showed a care for the building's community context – an approach resulting from it being a practice already deeply rooted in the fabric of the city of Manchester.

Hulme Crescents, at the time Britain's largest system-built housing estate

Right:
City Road Surgery, Hulme

CITY ROAD SURGERY
204

East elevation, Centenary Building,
University of Salford

While working on this small GP surgery, Hodder Associates was also tasked with a contrasting project – a significantly larger university commission. The fact that a relatively young practice could be commissioned to work at two such different scales showed something of the bullishness of Manchester and the city's approach to urban revival, which gave way to the fostering of the city's home-grown architectural talent. It also reflects the scale of Hodder's own ambitions for his practice.

In 1996 University College, Salford merged with the University of Salford to form a single institution. With this came the momentum for what to this day remains one of Hodder and Partners' key projects – the Centenary Building for the newly formed university's Departments of Spatial, Graphic and Industrial Design.

This scheme was designed in just 11 weeks in order to ensure that it was eligible for a European grant. The building, which contains studio and seminar spaces, is arranged in two blocks, with the facade bowing out to give space to an internal street punctured by galleries and bridges. The scheme went on to become a prototype for many later academic buildings.

For the University of Salford it was important to create not only a standalone building, but one which would help to link this new campus with the city. Therefore the Centenary Building project also included radical thinking about how the newly formed university would work, while attempting to link the disjointed campus with Manchester. It subtly faces out to the city, with its four-storey glazed block looking towards the city centre, while on the other side a new courtyard links the building with the site's existing Adelphi Building.

The building went on to win the inaugural Stirling Prize in 1996, and the judges described it as 'a dynamic, modern and sophisticated exercise in steel, glass and concrete'. The awarding of the first Stirling Prize to a Manchester building by a Manchester architect helped put the city firmly on the 20th century architectural map.

These two projects, at very different scales – one a modest doctors' surgery, another a significant university building – set out Hodder Associates' stall as a practice tackling projects on its own doorstep. They also demonstrated two very different approaches to regeneration. Through a university campus and through the wholescale rebuilding of tired housing stock, Manchester was changing.

However, in 1996 an event took place that shifted Manchester on its axis and would lead to the rebuilding of a whole district of the city centre. Not through slow, planned and careful urban regeneration – but as the result of a single, sudden and unpredictable event. On 15 June 1996, when an IRA bomb was detonated on Corporation Street – in the city's main commercial district – more than 100,000m² of shops and offices were destroyed within seconds. In that instant the city changed.

Occurring at a time when development in Manchester city centre was only just beginning to take off again after the recession of 1989, the bomb caused more than £700m worth of damage to the buildings surrounding the site of the blast, putting one of the city's key retail areas out of action for more than three years.

The devastation left by the Manchester bomb triggered one of the most ambitious and successful regeneration projects of its time. This tragedy and the subsequent need to repair the city – both physically

and emotionally – gave Manchester an opportunity to build, and build fast. Former Manchester City Council Chief Executive Sir Howard Bernstein made the point that 'The bomb gave the need for immediate renewal and provided opportunities for major regeneration in the city'. The city accelerated any planned development, in an act of defiance against the destruction caused by the IRA. In fact this provided a clean slate on which to masterplan some of the new developments that have subsequently contributed to Manchester earning the informal title of the UK's second city.

In the aftermath of the bombing, the city also launched a new development corporation, Manchester Millennium. It was modelled on Hulme Regeneration Ltd, the organisation responsible for kickstarting the regeneration of Hulme a couple of years earlier – and it is interesting how the earlier project acted as a blueprint for the transformation of the bomb-damaged city. Led by Alison Nimmo, who went on to become Chief Executive of the Crown Estate, Manchester Millennium played a central role in the regeneration and economic growth of the city centre, and has become one of the models followed by other cities such as Sheffield and Birmingham, which subsequently set up their own urban regeneration companies. However, Manchester Millennium could not have transformed the city on its own – it required a strong leadership within the city council – and this came from its Chief Executive Sir Howard Bernstein, and Leader of the Council Sir Richard Leese.

Corporation Street after the IRA bomb, June 1996

'The political leadership of Manchester has been key to its transformation. I can't think of another city where there has been such a stable leadership. Sir Howard and Sir Richard have harnessed public and private partnership, seeing this as a means to regeneration. It has created a background of opportunities that the city has been able to optimise.'
Stephen Hodder, 2017

In the immediate aftermath of the bomb Bernstein and Leese managed to secure around £100m of government money to aid the city, and once they had that they moved on to private investment. These private–public partnerships would prove vital to Manchester's transformation into a city to rival London, and would provide Hodder and Partners (as it now was) and other local architects with the work needed to maintain a practice in the North – an important factor in retaining creativity in the city. Manchester was one of the first cities to truly pioneer this form of engagement of the private sector to enable development throughout the city centre. By unlocking local authority pension funds, Manchester also initiated investment in housing. These methods of collaboration and development provided Manchester with the edge over other cities such as Leeds and Sheffield: they simply couldn't compete. What other cities did piecemeal, Manchester managed wholesale.

With this investment, and the immediate need for transformation of the bomb-damaged area, came a competition for the masterplan of this large part of the city centre. The competition was won by EDAW and local practice Ian Simpson Architects (now SimpsonHaugh and Partners), whose masterplan included a new square bordered by the Arndale Centre, the Corn Exchange and a new Marks & Spencer linked to St Ann's Square by a pedestrianised street. It also featured an extension to the north of the Arndale Centre with a large winter garden, a cultural building now known as the Printworks and a new transport interchange. The initial masterplan was followed by further masterplans designed to transform other areas of the city, including designs by Martha Schwartz for Exchange Square and BDP's Cathedral Gardens – the city's first new urban park for 70 years, and another winning bid by a Manchester-headquartered firm. The large-scale development needed after the bomb also acted as a form of practice for the city's future regeneration schemes, like that at Spinningfields, which included large-scale projects by Foster + Partners, Denton Corker Marshall and Aedas.

For Hodder and Partners, the rebuilding efforts after the bomb brought about another project on home turf, and a chance to contribute to the city's fast-paced transformation. In December 1997, 18 months after the blast, Hodder and Partners was named as the winner of a competition to reimagine the Corporation Street footbridge – part of Simpson's overall masterplan, and a project which was to become symbolic of Manchester's post-bomb renaissance.

The twisted glass-and-steel hyperbolic paraboloid structure was designed to link the new building housing Marks & Spencer and Selfridges with the existing Arndale Centre, stitching the city back together. It was another project where a local architect was given the chance to contribute to the rebuilding of their city, but with its iconic structure offering a symbol of hope its reach was far wider.

The new Corporation Street footbridge, an integral part of the overall masterplan for Manchester post-1996

For Manchester, much of the change seen after the IRA bomb was about getting people back into its city centre. Led by its city council and aided by developers such as Urban Splash, Manchester pioneered the movement of people back into urban centres from the suburbs by creating places where citizens could live, eat, work and play.

In Manchester the changes were happening as attitudes to urban regeneration were changing around the UK. Centred around Richard Rogers' government-commissioned 1999 report *Towards an Urban Renaissance*, urban regeneration was changing – and for the first time in a long time, urban design and planning was being used to tackle both the social and economic problems of the UK's post-industrial cities. Used as an exemplar, Manchester was set to be at the heart of these new thoughts about urban transformation and regeneration.

Manchester's transformation into a place of city living was spurred on by low interest rates, which allowed developers to build swathes of fashionable apartments, bringing young people into the city. During the 1980s, the number of people registered to vote in general elections in the City Centre ward averaged around 70, but by the early 2000s that figure had risen to closer to 20,000. After the conversions of the city's warehouses came the boom of high-rise development. Developers clamoured to build office, residential and retail schemes in the city, and at increasing height. For Hodder and Partners, this meant a development in its style, marrying with that of Manchester itself. It moved away from the quiet and contextual brick of early work at Hulme to more glassy schemes – and what could be argued to be a new contextual architecture of Manchester – with the building of offices at Piccadilly Place and Princess Street, and a new student housing tower on Great Marlborough Street.

4 Piccadilly Place, Manchester, one of six buildings within Argent's Piccadilly Place masterplan

Right:
55 Princess Street, Manchester, opposite Sir Alfred Waterhouse's Town Hall

Swinton
Swinton
Toronto
SNICKERS
GO NUTS
JCDecaux

The number of flat completions in Manchester city centre peaked at 3,000 in 2005. Like London, sales in the city centre were propped up by international investors buying off-plan and in bulk. By 2006 Manchester City Council had approved more than 20 towers in or around the city centre, representative of Manchester's changing urban environment. Build-to-rent is the latest phenomenon; at the end of 2016 roughly half of all planning consents in the city were for build-to-rent developments, and many of the city's architects were getting involved. In late 2016, Hodder and Partners completed a two-tower private rental sector housing scheme at the northern end of Cambridge Street, which consists of 282 apartments. Located on the bank of the River Medlock, the scheme brings life to a derelict horseshoe-shaped plot which was defined in the area's masterplan (drawn up by Sir Terry Farrell) as being a landmark gateway site for the city. Split into two blocks arranged around a courtyard, the development attempts to link visually with the adjacent Grade II-listed Chorlton Mill and a new apartment building to the east.

Many of those involved in Manchester's transformation from a heady mix of musical culture and nightlife to a city where investors flock to its glass towers have remained in the city – from Hodder and Partners, which has developed alongside the changing environment, to Urban Splash's Tom Bloxham, who started out selling posters in the city's Affleck's Palace and has gone on to become known as one of the UK's most innovative and successful property developers. Indeed even Tony Wilson, the founder of Factory Records, was advising on urban regeneration before his death in 2007. The attitudes of the city – its council and its community – gave people with an interest the chance to get stuck in and play a part in how their home city was planned and shaped.

No. 1 Cambridge Street, Manchester

In April 2017, Hodder and Partners won planning permission for a new RHS garden and visitor centre at the site of the former Worsley New Hall on the outskirts of Salford. The centre, alongside the BBC's northern headquarters and developments happening at the university, could put Salford on the map, seeing it emerge from beneath the shadows of its brasher next-door neighbour, Manchester. It was no secret that Bernstein had always wanted the BBC's northern home to be in Manchester proper, and the decision to move it to Salford angered him. It was this scheme – the BBC's Media City at Salford Quays – that really kickstarted investment in the area. And so with Bernstein's retirement from the city council comes a new era of change. According to Stephen Hodder, projects like RHS Garden Bridgewater 'signal its growth and ambition as a city in its own right'. For Hodder and Partners, it is another project on the practice's own patch, and a return to the area where things really took off for the firm in 1996 with the Stirling Prize win. The Centenary Building itself is also going through significant changes, almost 22 years after it was completed. The campus, having been built up over the years, is taking stock and shifting to reflect the changes in academic teaching methods and university funding. Again, as it did in the beginning.

Both Salford and the city of Manchester have provided a place for Hodder Associates and then Hodder and Partners to grow and thrive, embedded in the northernness of its oeuvre. The practice is one of a number of larger local firms that are often behind the city's big schemes. Look at any development in Manchester's city centre and it will probably bear the badge of the practices of Hodder, Simpson or Roger Stephenson – each has developed alongside the city while forging very different paths for themselves.

The welcome building,
RHS Garden Bridgewater

It is a symbol of Manchester itself – as a hub of creativity – that it can support so many architectural firms, from the large to the small. But without the 1996 bomb and the subsequent need for fast regeneration brought on by the tragedy, would these practices have thrived in the same way? What is clear is that Manchester has defined a generation of local practices, each of which decided to make this northern city its home.

When Manchester's regeneration and development is contextualised against a background of creativity in other areas like art, music and urban culture, it all comes together. The city's renaissance didn't just come in the form of new buildings and masterplans; it also manifested itself in popular culture, from club nights to independent shopping. It was fortunate that all the conditions that allowed for positive changes to develop came together in the late 1990s – and since then the city has seen significant growth, placing itself at the heart of debates about regeneration. Manchester has become the city that others look to for clues about how to develop their tired, post-industrial centres.

Hodder and Partners' affinity with Manchester is perhaps typified by its work at St Michael's, a strategically important development which connects Spinningfields with the civic core. Hodder was initially brought in by Manchester City Council as an independent design adviser to the controversial project led by ex-footballers Gary Neville and Ryan Giggs. The apparent lack of contextualisation, and concerns over the future of the historic Sir Ralph Abercrombie public house in Bootle Street and the nearby neoclassical police station (1937), which were set to be demolished, alarmed citizens and heritage bodies alike. Is it just a coincidence that

Duncan House, Stratford, East London

Hodder was brought in on this project, or is it a case of local knowledge prevailing? The revised proposals demonstrate how the practice's history in Manchester enable it to negotiate tensions between maintaining the city's Victorian heritage and its desire to move forward as a 21st century powerhouse. For Hodder and Partners, its long-term compassion for its home has paid off. As it continues to work in the city, the lessons learned mean it is a practice trusted not only in Manchester but also further afield.

Hodder and Partners was a practice in its infancy as Manchester was coming to the fore, and its development has run in tandem with that of the city. Its projects have grown in size alongside the ambitions of the city itself, and this has fostered a deep understanding of Manchester as a place, which can be seen in the contextual nature of the work.

St Michael's, Manchester

ROB
GREGORY

ARTICULATING LEGIBILITY, CRAFT, PEOPLE AND PLACES

'We require from buildings two kinds of goodness: first, the doing their practical duty well: then that they be graceful and pleasing in doing it.'
John Ruskin, *The Stones of Venice*, 1851

This piece focuses on an approach to construction that has guided Hodder and Partners' work for almost 30 years. Tracing its roots back to the professional and academic context of Stephen Hodder's formative years, this essay merges parallel influences from the time: inspirations behind Deyan Sudjic's seminal exhibition and publication *Norman Foster, Richard Rogers, James Stirling: New Directions in British Architecture* in 1986, shifts in public perception agitated by the Prince of Wales's *Vision of Britain* in 1989, and the enduring influence of academic lessons from Hodder's time at Manchester University. It also mirrors precisely the formative years of the author's own career in architecture, and as such represents a significant strand of influence, tracing as it does the career of an architect who has been hitting the headlines for almost 30 years.

The timing of Hodder's graduation in 1981 was significant for a number of reasons. First, it meant that the young architect entered the profession when British architecture was escaping the doldrums of the 1970s, experiencing that upward trajectory celebrated by Sudjic in the Royal Academy's first architecture exhibition in 40 years. Architecture's creative landscape was more fertile than it had been for some time, enabling architects like Hodder to chart their own course. A new generation rode the wave that had been set in motion by British high-tech, with contemporaries like Allies and Morrison, David Chipperfield and Stanton Williams harnessing the momentum with new architectural twists and turns that would enrich the country's architectural culture. For Hodder, his new architectural moves demonstrated a refreshing agility in relating construction to context.

Before discussing the detail of Hodder and Partners' approach, however, the influence of the practice's predecessors should not go unnoted. In relation to British architecture's all-important new direction, Stephen Hodder is first to acknowledge how the previous generation had done much of the hard work. At the forefront of British high-tech and the renaissance it brought was Norman Foster, who unsurprisingly ranks high in Hodder's field of reference, with parallels that go beyond personal ambitions to emulate the success of his fellow Manchester alumnus. References to Foster are present throughout his academic and professional career, as Hodder describes time spent completing his Part III with Building Design Partnership (BDP) as two years of trying to emulate Foster's silver sheds. Thirty years on, Foster's influence remains present, not only in his work but also in how Hodder presents himself. This can be appreciated when you walk into his canalside premises in Manchester, which bear hallmarks of Foster's impressive Riverside Studio in London, albeit on a more human scale.

Understanding that legibility is more than the sum of its parts

While comparisons with Foster have not always been appreciated by Hodder himself, they do come with the territory that he occupies. He chose to study in Manchester on the recommendation of a college tutor who was a fan of Foster's work and, as described elsewhere in this publication, it was the Sainsbury Centre that inspired Hodder's faith in modern architecture. What Hodder and his contemporaries did differently was to acknowledge that while Sudjic's thesis had demonstrated that in the hands of Foster and Rogers almost anything was possible in creative and technological terms, in response to shifts in public perception and Prince Charles's *Vision of Britain* the next generation of British architects would need to address demands for quieter and more contextual displays of innovation.

Fortunately for Hodder, this is where academic influences served him well – through the tuition of Ronald Brunskill, who taught him about the vernacular, and through the school's encouragement in developing an appreciation for Scandinavian sensibilities, as shown in the work of architects like Peter Aldington. The most significant influence, however, came from Hodder's research into Arne Jacobsen, and his emerging admiration for the legibility of the great Dane's expression of architectural elements. As part of a conservation design programme led by tutor Derek Dearden, Hodder had been directed to a recently deposited PhD thesis by Rod Hackney, who had spent two years working for Jacobsen. And so from this moment on, Hodder's career-long interest in St Catherine's College, Oxford was born. A decade later this would pay dividends, when Hodder's admiration and understanding of that place helped him secure one of three key projects that would catapult him from obscurity to national prominence.

Articulating community – Colne Swimming Pool (1992)

As Hodder's first solo project, Colne Swimming Pool set the tone for much that followed, bringing the young architect the first in a long run of major competition wins, national design awards and coverage in the national press. It also represented

East elevation, Colne Swimming Pool, Lancashire

a significant threshold in the evolution of Hodder Associates' approach, marking the culmination of a nine-year period of gestation – and the all-important transition into realising his own designs.

Unsurprisingly, this building displays more high-tech references than any that followed, embodying as it did the exuberance of projects like Foster's 1982 Renault showroom in Swindon from the decade before. This was to be expected, not only because this was the first opportunity for Hodder to assemble a high-calibre design team, but also because the time had come for him to make his mark, exercise his own ambitions and deploy his own fastidious attention to detail.

Colne was much more than an expression of youthful enthusiasm, though, encapsulating as it did Hodder's response to the problem of how to reconcile high-tech sensibilities with a renewed interest in place and history. No doubt inspired by the work of those all-important predecessors – Hopkins at Lord's and Foster at Nîmes – Hodder's very first building was to be his manifesto, demonstrating how mixed modes of heavy and lightweight construction can respond specifically to context and the ground, and how architecture could derive character from a direct response to the pragmatic needs of the brief.

As an extension to one of Nicholas Grimshaw's 1984 SASH sports halls, the available triangular site was too small to follow the Sports Council's standard guidelines on how to extend the original, so Hodder carved up all the available ground by fusing the orthogonal grid of Grimshaw's standard box with the axis of Colne's Victorian streetscape, oriented 18 degrees south of west. Through this, he took command of the site, unifying the pool and walls – which were anchored to the ground – with the more expressive technical roof, in a three-dimensional expression of geometric resolution. Divided into six bays, defined by two

Roofline of Colne Swimming Pool

axes and with roof planes that fall in two directions, the building was expressed as a complex sawtooth arrangement that terminates at its prow in a space that Hodder intended as an urban clearing.

While more conventional contextual observations supported the strategy, with references made by architect and critics to echoes of the distant hills and the sharp grey silhouette of the townscape, it could be argued that these have only limited relevance to a building on a flat site that hunkers down beside the railway station. What this building did most convincingly was demonstrate how architects should construct in context, and how rigorous responses to pragmatic concerns can produce buildings of character and presence. Working with Anthony Hunts, the building became an essay in how architecture and engineering should come together, in a structure that derives its form and function from contextual and pragmatic constraints. Its increases in span and cranks in plan and elevation are masterfully controlled to produce subtle increases in truss depths, window sizes and roof pitches. It all finds its balance within that all-important anchor column that roots the building in place, coming together to heighten the dramatic effect of swimming down the pool, on the axis of one of the town's main streets and with an enlarging vista of townscape gently revealed.

Not bad for his first attempt, the headlines could have said, as in a curious twist of fate, Hodder and Foster shared the podium as joint winners of the 1992 Royal Fine Art Commission/Sunday Times Building of the Year award, with Colne and Foster's Sackler Galleries both exemplifying new relationships between modernism and powerful context. Both schemes were also praised for their finely tuned contextual responses to the nuts and bolts of structure, access, servicing and circulation.

Articulating place – St Catherine's College, Oxford, Phase I (1994)

Following the publicity surrounding Colne Swimming Pool, Hodder won his second key commission at St Catherine's College, Oxford, having been invited to compete in a design competition alongside 4 notable competitors including David Chipperfield, John McAslan, Julian Wickham and Dixon Jones.

In many people's eyes, as a virtual unknown he was the rank outsider. However, while his winning scheme underwent a radical rethink post competition, Hodder proved to be convincing and persuasive, communicating his passion for and understanding of Jacobson's buildings sufficiently well to win the commission and galvanise a relationship with the college that endures to this day.

It wasn't an easy transition, though, and the burden of responsibility quickly took hold, as Hodder recalled when describing the sleepless nights and gut-wrenching anxiety he experienced while unpicking his initial proposal to radically remodel Jacobsen's squash courts. In the end, pragmatism prevailed over absolutism in his multiple-award-winning Phase I buildings, which added 54 new en-suite bedrooms and three new staircases to Jacobsen's apparently 'complete' composition.

Hodder was aware of Reyner Banham's criticism of Jacobson's 'motel', but based his response on his own critical appraisal of the existing context, and on how – in his view – St Catherine's scarcely responds to its surroundings, cutting itself off from Oxford. He also saw how Jacobsen had paid little attention to the nature or history of the site, to necessary differences between public and private, to orientation, or to the relationship between inside and out. As fundamental

St Catherine's College, Oxford, Phase I

Left:
Staircase 17,
St Catherine's College, Oxford, Phase I

as these flaws may sound, however, his admiration for Jacobsen's rigorous approach to order, structure, materials and detailing is clear to see in the final approach, which presents a composition that strikes the perfect balance between referential adherence to a set of established rules, and the sort of creative innovation that you would expect of a young and ambitious emerging talent.

Having abandoned plans to wrap residential accommodation around the existing squash courts to the south-west of the site, Hodder's challenge to himself was to create a new gateway to the site by confronting one of the key edges of Jacobsen's 'universal plane'. To the south, the existing college buildings virtually ignored the presence of the Holywell Mill Stream, so Hodder composed a three-storey, three-bay terrace that responded to the dual axes of river and grid, with the upper two floors extending Jacobsen's original planning grid, set above a ground floor that cranks its land-side facade to run parallel to the stream beyond.

In a quieter articulation of solid and void than that seen at Colne, Hodder then added layers of expression. First, he completely reinvented the college staircases that Jacobsen had embedded in the relative depths of his linear plans. These form a trio of dynamic and daylit spaces that express the divergent geometries of the two axes, and emphasise the contrast between the shared glazed staircases and the private enclosed study blocks to which they give access. At the most detailed scale, a second layer of expression was created by extending the rhythm of Jacobsen's full-height glass panels in crisp stainless steel, and framing a single deep-set pane to improve the privacy and environmental stability of each new room. This was successful to such a degree that Hodder's demonstrable ability to construct in context led to

Staircase 22,
St Catherine's College, Oxford,
Phase II

Right:
St Catherine's College, Oxford,
Phase I

his retention by the college, and his subsequent appointments to convert the Junior Common Room courtyard into a lecture theatre, to refurbish all 16 of Jacobsen's original staircases and 320 study rooms, and also to complete a second phase of new-build accommodation, with Project Associate Mark Emms, that added an additional seven staircases and 131 new rooms.

Articulating function – Centenary Building (1996)

By the time his third major commission was secured, Hodder had become established as a leading member of a small group of uncompromising modernists who were operating outside of the longstanding architectural cliques of London, in the heart of Manchester's hard-edged and rapidly changing Castlefield quarter. He was working as part of a generation of ambitious and entrepreneurial architects and developers that included peers such as Ian Simpson, Stephenson Bell, Urban Splash and ShedKM, but none of them realised just how significant their combined efforts would be in the gradual (and ongoing) decentralisation of British architecture and regeneration, in a move that pre-dates any mention of the so-called 'northern powerhouse'. And little did Hodder know, in relation to this building, just how highly his efforts would be rewarded – as this low-budget, standalone faculty building for the recently merged University of Salford and University College, Salford, was destined to become the nation's first Stirling Prize winner.

Determined to demonstrate a radical construction-led alternative to the sort of faceless multipurpose education buildings developed in the 1980s, Hodder's Centenary Building (Project Architect Christian Male) made a huge impact, anticipating a number

The Centenary Building, University of Salford

of subsequent shifts in the architecture of the 21st century university. It achieved this through a focus on the now-commonplace aspirations for efficiency, flexibility and social engineering (i.e. how a building can improve social relationships) that are so clearly articulated at the heart of its plan.

Articulation of parts was key to the success of the building, relating to the university's strict requirement to be able to relocate departments in future. The solution had to accommodate cellular offices, laboratories, workshops, teaching spaces and large, well-lit studios; a scenario that was tested even before completion, when the mid-development decision was made to swap departments around. Due to the clarity of the structure, the efficiency of its plan and the legibility and social role of its common spine, this decision caused some delay but led to little disruption of the overall design.

Beyond the context of the education faculty typology, the building also performs a placemaking role, creating the fourth side of a courtyard shared with the Adelphi Building, a former office and factory building that dates from 1915. This reinforces a notional axis between the two city centres of Manchester and Salford, which is articulated within the building by an internal street that runs between the teaching and administrative/support spaces.

Along this fault line, concrete crosswalls are staggered, creating a dynamic tension between each side of the gorge-like street, and an asymmetry that reaches its maximum where the plan billows to accommodate lecture theatres and open-plan studios.

Simple in plan but with a more intricate section, the final layer of articulation comes with Hodder's now trademark use of concrete, glass blocks and stainless steel, all of which serve dual purposes on this site

Detail, South elevation, The Centenary Building, University of Salford

as hardwearing and robust specifications. This articulation is composed in response to each of the building's four orientations: closing down to the rear, opening up to the courtyard, and expressing the building's layered section at each end. Inside, the interiors add a further layer of spatial articulation – opening up the glass-fronted offices, studios, seminar rooms and teaching spaces, placing the key activities on show, and encouraging students and colleagues to drop in.

Local heroics – demonstrating the value of making, craft and detail

Despite the architectural whirlwind that saw these three key commissions propel Hodder from obscurity to headline-grabbing new talent, the young architect was determined to keep his feet firmly on the ground, and to establish a robust business in his adopted city of Manchester. While the country continued its steady crawl out of the recession of the early 1990s, Hodder did not simply chase the new generation of lottery-funded flagship projects. Instead, he chose to focus on a number of carefully selected local projects that would enable him to demonstrate a commitment to the importance of placemaking and to architecture's ability to contribute to local identity. While not an exhaustive representation of this contribution, the following trio of small-scale projects usefully illustrates how Hodder honed his interest in a place-based approach to construction while tackling local design codes, developing a new approach to refurbishment and interiors, and resolving one of his most overt exercises in structural expressionism, all of which also show his commitment to the articulation of craft and materials.

Interior 'street', Centenary Building, showing the glazed tutor's offices, and studios

Articulating typology – City Road Surgery (1996)

Even though it was not Hodder's first project, City Road Surgery is a typical manifesto building for a young architect, taking as it does an existing typology and making a radically new form of building. Inspired by modernism's ambitious healthcare schemes, for example by Lubetkin and others immediately after the Second World War, and supported by the patronage of a committed and visionary GP client, Hodder's modest building belies its modest size to make a significant contribution to the typology. It is a pragmatic response to conflicting requirements of security and the need to provide abundant natural light and air. It also makes a contribution in terms of placemaking, realised through the manner in which it mediates the scale of the existing terrace, and resolves the orientation of dual frontages that address street and park.

Through its resolution of the two core obligations, the building attains a unique formal and material quality, which has been credited as an extension to the great Mancunian architectural tradition through its expert handling of brick walls, glass blocks, clerestory windows and architectural metalwork. These are unified under its distinctive gullwing roof, fabricated as a stressed-skin monocoque and bolted together on site in 1200mm plywood sections. This articulates an important route through the building from the more public waiting rooms to the south to the more private consulting rooms to the north, fronting on to the park.

City Road Surgery from St George's Park, Hulme

Left:
Roof detail, City Road Surgery, Hulme

Articulating new and old – CUBE (1998)

CUBE in central Manchester followed two years later, and this gave Hodder the opportunity to make an overt contribution to the culture of architecture in the city, as both a founding trustee and architect of the city's new Centre for the Understanding of the Built Environment.

By radically transforming the outdated and uninviting old Building Centre, in this instance Hodder's interest in materials and construction responded to the context of a number of as-found interiors, through the architect's now trademark manipulation of form, surface and texture.

While this architectural approach has since become widespread in Manchester, at the time Hodder's intervention at CUBE was highly innovative and ideally suited to the purposes of a centre of excellence in architecture and design. Through its extensive but intricately planned interiors, a range of unique original details were juxtaposed with the clarity of Hodder's new plan in a carefully choreographed sequence of orientation and exhibition spaces that celebrate red-brick arched openings, carved stone cornices, cast-iron columns and original joinery.

Since then this highly articulated approach to restoration has been described as the Manchester Style, and it has become so popular that people now design new buildings that somewhat counterintuitively resemble Hodder's early composition of contemporary insertions within an existing historic setting.

Interior and details, CUBE gallery, Manchester

Articulating structure – Corporation Street Footbridge (1999)

As the final example in this trio of small-scale local interventions, Hodder won the competition to design a new footbridge over Corporation Street in Manchester as part of a significant civic project to repair the city's commercial and retail centre following the devastation of the 1996 IRA bomb. Hodder's response was to articulate the structure in a manner that would optically correct the level change across the span, by stretching and twisting a hyperbolic paraboloid structure across the street. By overlaying two spirals of structural steel, with tension rods and compression members twisting in opposite directions, the composite weblike structure simultaneously provides a transparent point of transition between two retail centres and a new landmark for the city. It also reasserts Hodder's high-tech roots, with a constellation of steel, glass and timber connections all meticulously detailed and coordinated.

Net-like steel structure, Corporation Street footbridge, Manchester

Left:
Walking across Corporation Street footbridge

Upscaling – showing how buildings can engage people and places

Hodder was now established as both a national player and an influential local design advocate and businessman, so it was inevitable that his work would need to address the issue of scale: not only as a result of his emerging popularity, but also due to the influence of a recovering economy and a renewed interest in urban regeneration. For Hodder this led to a number of large-scale commissions, briefly explored here in a second trio of local projects that demonstrate how architecture can articulate the relationship between people and places, in contrasting contexts of landscape, streetscape and cityscape.

Articulating landscape –
National Wildflower Centre (2000)

The National Wildflower Centre came first, as one of many high-profile lottery-funded projects commissioned to mark the dawn of the 21st century.

Just 30 miles outside Manchester, the 35-acre Court Hey Park site presented a very different context from Hodder's typical architectural habitat. However, he was quick to respond to the disparate nature of the landscape with trademark sensitivity, understanding and clarity, identifying a clear separation in the quality of the landscape between the east and west of the park, and a dead zone running through the middle.

In response to a brief that called for a contemporary building that would reflect the centre's principal mission to conserve natural habitats for future generations, Hodder, with collaborator Maurice Shapero, deployed his building as if it were a new garden wall, occupying the fallow strip of land between two more established landscape settings. Incorporating fragments of a Victorian stable block, ranger's hut and walled garden, the new 4m-wide and 160m-long inhabited wall articulated the latent order of the site in one decisive architectural move that forms both destination and threshold. It provides essential visitor facilities within its depth, and creates a number of key vantage points from which visitors can view the centre's activities.

While simple at a strategic level, Hodder's singular choice of reinforced concrete heightens the impact of numerous points of articulation that occur along the building's length, separated from the ground with cantilevers, cutouts and a continuous roof terrace framing site-wide views for all to enjoy. The building acts as threshold, enclosure and link.

Interior, National Wildflower Centre

Café, National Wildflower Centre, Knowsley

Overleaf:
Entrance and café, National Wildflower Centre, Knowsley

55 Princess Street, Manchester, *in situ*

Old and new, 55 Princess Street

Left:
Entrance, 55 Princess Street

Articulating streetscape – 55 Princess Street (2006)

Back in town, in the heart of the city's extensive conservation area, Hodder's 55 Princess Street demonstrates the architect's ability to respond to a streetscape, while providing over 78,000 sq ft of office space for the commercial development sector. This was achieved by allowing each elevation to respond to its immediate neighbours, both through its formal composition and the detailing of its materials.

Its principal frontage features a projecting zinc box at first-floor level that recalls the composition of its predecessor and is at a scale more sympathetic to passing pedestrians, while its seven-storey glazed core signals the building's entrance and helps to resolve historic steps in the street's building line.

To the rear, where the building establishes new levels behind the retained facades of 36–40 Kennedy Street, Hodder articulated the building's cross-section by creating a full-height lightwell that emphasises the phases of construction, allows historic fenestration levels to coexist with new floor slabs, and celebrates the passage of light and air between new and old.

Articulating cityscape – Cambridge Street (2016)

Finally, when commissioned to design an entire urban block, Hodder's articulate response to formal and elevational composition prevailed as the key generating device in the design of one of the practice's most recently completed projects, Cambridge Street, south of the city centre.

On a derelict horseshoe-shaped plot, bound on two sides by the River Medlock, the 282-unit residential scheme is arranged in two opposing towers that rise from a split-level podium car park. Balanced in height and relative disposition, the 28- and 19-storey towers complement one another when viewed from across the city, successfully de-massing the development and responding to the desire for the site to act as a new landmark gateway to the city.

At a more detailed level, the architect added levels of articulation to the facades through the modelling of external forms and surfaces, with cores expressed in bronze powder-coated aluminium sheafs, verticality accentuated by two-storey slit-windows in the centres of the facades, and flush two-storey balconies that frame deep external recesses; all of which demonstrate a precision of detail that we have come to expect from this architect.

Conclusion

While not intended to draw clever conclusions or make predictions, the three-by-three structure of this essay threads together nine completed projects and three key themes that have shaped almost three decades of work. It shows the practice's formative and headline-grabbing seminal projects at Colne, Salford and St Catherine's, Oxford – where Hodder's architecture emerged from the legibility of each component part – through to the trio of lovingly crafted small-scale projects in his home city of Manchester that relied on the articulation of craft and detail, and finally three landmark projects which depended on the architect's ability to reconcile the relationship between people and places at the scale of landscape, streetscape and cityscape.

Hodder's story is far from over. One of the main advantages of having started to accumulate such an accomplished portfolio of work at such an early age is that today, at the age of 61, with partner Claire and a

The complementary towers of No. 1 Cambridge Street, Manchester

CINTOSH & Cº LIMITED
INDIA RUBBER WO

talented group of directors and associates at his side, Stephen Hodder still has a long, prosperous and creatively ambitious future ahead of him. In the decades to come, those who share an interest in a broader culture of British architecture beyond that which presides in the capital, will, like me, look forward with confidence to watch Hodder's sustained evolution of these architectural themes, and to witness the completion of an increasingly mature and sophisticated series of buildings from a practice that has consciously avoided huge leaps in its creative and commercial development.

And so in this spirit, before we end this brief but timely review of his work, we suggest that you take the time to study the plans, sections, elevations and details of one of the practice's most recently completed projects, St Clare's in Oxford, which serves as a watershed project by bringing Hodder's journey full circle and returning him to the context of Oxford, where he so dramatically burst on to the scene in 1994. Three decades on, just as then, this project demonstrates in abundance how Hodder continues to care passionately about the continuity and culture of architectural excellence: articulating the legibility of each component and junction; honouring the craft of materials and making; and expressing the relationship between people and places. Long may this architectural mission continue, in an industry where these exemplary sensibilities are increasingly under threat.

Art studio interior, St Clare's, Oxford

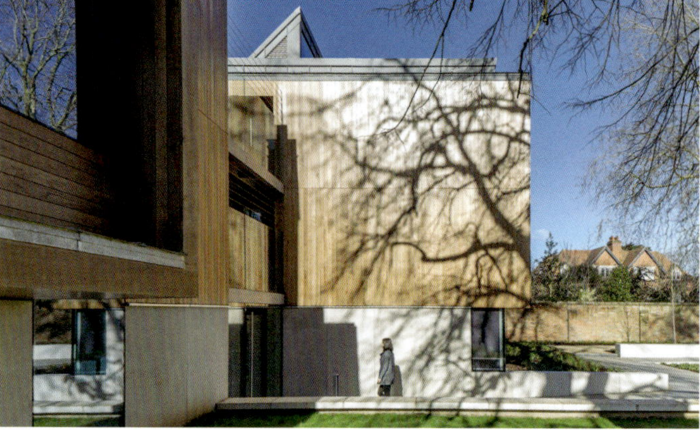

The quadrangle, St Clare's, Oxford

Entrance, garden pavilion, St Clare's, Oxford

Art studio exterior, St Clare's, Oxford

CONTRIBUTORS

PETER WALKER

Peter Walker is an architect and Professor of Construction Science and Management at the University of Salford. Throughout his working life he has combined architectural practice with teaching, writing, research and consultancy. He was previously Professor of Architecture and Head of the Belfast School of Architecture, taught at Newcastle University, and was director of a major health care practice and of an international design consultancy.

He has written and contributed to a number of books and academic papers, been appointed as a consultant to the Egyptian Government Building Research Council and an independent adviser to the Architects' Registration Board, and is an external examiner and visiting professor at universities in the UK and the Lebanon.

HUGH PEARMAN

Hugh Pearman is a London-based architecture and design critic who edits the *RIBA Journal* and writes for many other media ranging from *Royal Academy Magazine* to *The Spectator*. For 30 years he was the architecture critic of *The Sunday Times*, in which role he helped to establish the Stirling Prize for architecture – the first winner of which, in 1996, was Stephen Hodder's Centenary Building at the University of Salford. Hugh has written and contributed to many books, including his bestselling *Contemporary World Architecture*, published by Phaidon. An Honorary Fellow of the RIBA, he was Visiting Professor in Architecture at the Royal College of Art in 2015.

TONY CHAPMAN

Tony Chapman is not a trained architect, but in 2010 the RIBA made him an Honorary Fellow for his contributions to architecture as a writer, film-maker and the RIBA's Head of Awards, a job he left in 2016. He is now a full-time writer and architectural consultant.

Previously, as a BBC TV producer, he made documentaries about architecture and the environment – including the modernists' riposte to the Prince of Wales's *Vision of Britain*.

He is the author of over 20 books, including two on the Stirling Prize, a children's book on architecture and three novels. He is working on a book with Peter Zumthor, and another on built and unbuilt buildings. He writes for the *Architects' Journal*, the *RIBA Journal* and *C20 Magazine*. He has judged the RIBA Awards, the RIBA Lubetkin Prize, the Mies Prize, the Manser Medal, the AJ Small Project Awards, the AJ Retrofit Awards and the Architects' Journal Awards.

LAURA MARK

Laura Mark is an award-winning architecture critic, curator, film-maker and designer. Trained as an architect, Laura spent five years in architectural practice before joining the editorial team of the *Architects' Journal*. She went on to become the magazine's digital editor, where she led the redesign of the *AJ's* website, and later became architecture editor. During her time at the magazine Laura won numerous awards for her work including title of IBP's Multi-media Journalist of the Year in both 2015 and 2016. She has gone on to contribute to a number of books on architecture and the built environment. Laura began film-making in 2015, and the subsequent work she has produced is concerned with creating a visual understanding of the feeling and delight of architecture. Her film, *Zaha Hadid: A Legacy* (2017), was shown at the London Architecture Film Festival, the Milan Design Film Festival and the New York Architecture and Design Film Festival.

ROB GREGORY

Rob Gregory is an award-winning architect, editor and curator whose work has appeared in internationally published books, newspapers and journals. Having worked on key projects with Feilden Clegg Bradley Studios, Hopkins and Allies and Morrison, Rob's career took a detour from conventional practice when he joined the *Architectural Review* in 2003. Promoted to Senior Editor he spent over ten years travelling the world, producing celebrated editions on emerging architecture from India, Japan, Australia and beyond. Returning to work in his home city of Bristol, the next five years were spent as a curator and design advocate, running the Architecture Centre's public programme alongside a number of other consultant appointments. These included lead roles on the Royal Academy and British Council architecture programmes and extended terms on the South West Design Review Panel, Bristol Urban Design Forum, and the RIBA's National Awards Group. Consolidating all that he has learned, Rob returned to practice in 2016 while maintaining the post of University of Bath Teaching Fellow that he has held since 2003.

INDEX

Page numbers in **bold** refer to images.

T

U

V

W

Z